THE WOMEN OF MURIEL SPARK

THE WOMEN OF MURIEL SPARK

Judy Sproxton

Constable · London

First published in Great Britain 1992
by Constable & Company Limited
3 The Lanchesters, 162 Fulham Palace Road
London W6 9ER
Copyright © Judy Sproxton 1992
The right of Judy Sproxton to be
identified as the author of this work has been
asserted by her in accordance with the
Copyright, Designs and Patents Act 1988
ISBN 0 09 471380 4
Set in Linotron Ehrhardt by
Falcon Typographic Art Ltd,
Fife, Scotland
Printed in Great Britain by
St Edmundsbury Press Ltd
Bury St Edmunds, Suffolk

A CIP catalogue record for this book
is available from the British Library

This book was written for
Constance Swan, my mother

Contents

INTRODUCTION

The greatest irony in Muriel Spark's fiction is its success. Peter Owen, the publisher for whom she worked in 1958, has said that she was amazed by the warm reception accorded to her first novel, *The Comforters*. She had thought of herself as a poet and a biographer; writing fiction had never attracted her. Then, already well known in literary circles, she was commissioned by Alan Maclean of Macmillan to write a novel. She embarked on this project in the winter of 1955. The book turned out to be a revelation about her resources. The sensitivity to words and to their hidden wit which had dynamized her poetry found a new medium in the novel: the very power of words and their hold on the mind became the major theme of this one. Her elegance of phrase, her intellectual control and capacity for stringent organization of material had already made of her a sound and efficient biographer; these talents enabled her to construct in her novel an unpredictable plot with many possibilities to exploit, many meaningful details to retain, and a forceful resolution.

Until recently, there has been no reliable source from which to derive an account of Spark's early life. Derek Stanford's brief biographical study of her which he published in 1963 has been discredited by Spark herself. Fortunately, Spark has in recent years embarked on her own autobiography.* Two sections of this have appeared in *The New Yorker*; the material they contain

1* To be published by Constable in 1992.

is invaluable to the student of Spark's work, since it makes clear how many features of Spark's intrinsic personality and the experience of her childhood contribute to the substance of her novels.

Muriel Spark was born in Edinburgh in 1918; her father was a Scottish Jew and her mother was English. Spark was conscious of the fact that her mother dressed rather differently and indeed *was* rather different from the other women of her age in Edinburgh; apart from her nationality her mother had a nervous condition and could not be left alone in the house. Spark says that she herself accepted this idea 'robustly'; she clearly had a happy family life, and greatly admired her father whom she inwardly acknowledged for his understanding of child psychology when on one occasion, after his daughter had been crying, he wiped her dolls' eyes. Her mother would take her visiting, which she loved. Children were expected to sit quietly on such occasions, but Spark recalls being glad of this since she loved to listen. She was clearly fascinated by personalities at an early age. She was thrilled when visitors came to her parents' house, retaining vivid visual memories of the visitors, and mental records of their stories and circumstances. Even people she did not meet fired her imagination: her paternal grandmother, for example, of whom she had only heard, featured in Spark's imagination as reading her Bible and sitting on her long hair at the same time, since she was reputed to have done both. She also 'imagined' Emmeline Pankhurst, of whom her maternal grandmother spoke.

Spark's own powers of perception as a child are obviously a source for the way in which children are frequently portrayed in her work. One need only cite the baby in *The First Year of my Life* who smiled for the first time when Asquith broadcast his statement that the 1914–18 war had 'cleansed and purged the world'. The smile was of course ironic, and it is the irony of the child's perception, seeing beyond the fatuous myth of adults, that Spark uses to dissolve the mystique of adult hypocrisy. In this story, the child's smile is, in a sense, metaphorical. However, in

later works, such as *The Prime of Miss Jean Brodie*, much of the
narrative is expressed from the viewpoint of children and their
insights are in turn romantic and devastating. Muriel Spark's
account of her own childhood gives an example of the integrity
of her early youth; her much admired Aunt Gertie took her to
see Florrie Ford, the music hall star, which was an overwhelming
experience for her. Her parents, however, who had been at a race
meeting, greeted the news of their trip with gales of laughter.
Spark observes that she can never to this day understand why
they should have responded in this way; she implies that she
handled her incomprehension with dignity, even at this age, and
stood by her original pleasure in the outing.

Spark was excited by the tales she heard of her acquaintances
and of her family (her father ran away to sea at the age of fourteen
and got as far as the Orkneys, whence he was returned, very sea
sick). However, there was a sober side to her early experience,
which indicates how, without being a consciously political writer,
Spark was aware from the outset of class divisions in society. She
tells how she would see poor men and women singing for pennies
on the back green, behind her house. 'I was aware', she writes,
'that others suffered. Poor as we certainly were, there were others
greatly poorer than we.' She notices barefoot children 'clustered
round smelly pubs'. Together with an acknowledgement of
the problems life held for some, she appears to have had at
the same time a sense of privilege that her own life was so
'abundant'. She remembers it as 'crammed with people and
amazing information'. She is still grateful for these rich early
days in which she was 'prepared and briefed to my full capacity'.
This resulted, she declared, from being integrated into adult life
rather than being 'cozied' in a nursery.

The second part of her recollections of childhood is concerned with her school days. She acknowledges with passion
the importance to her of these years, which stimulated her
intellect and which also fed her response to people, already
so well developed in her pre-school years. The school she
attended was James Gillespie's High School for girls, founded

by an admirer of the Covenanters ('worthy bearers of Bible and sword who rebelled against the imposition of the English liturgy in the 17th century'). Officially the school was Presbyterian, but Tolerance was the prevailing religion of her day 'always with a puritanical slant'. The overwhelming feature of Spark's account of her school days is the description of her teacher, Miss Christina Kay. Miss Kay is acknowledged as the source of Spark's infamous character, Miss Jean Brodie, and indeed, the similarities are unmistakable. Spark relates how she started to write about Miss Kay at the age of ten, so inspired was she by the heady mixture of culture, romance and incisive comment which her school teacher's life relayed to her. Like Miss Brodie, Christina Kay adorned her classroom walls with reproductions of early Renaissance paintings; equally, she placed there newspaper cuttings about Mussolini's troops.

The way in which Spark developed the character of Miss Brodie shows how fertile this contact with Christina Kay's forceful personality was to be in her literary life. On a personal level, both she and her friend Frances were encouraged and nurtured by Christina Kay, who insisted that they should 'benefit from all that Edinburgh had to offer'. Miss Kay was a member of those post-war spinsters, deprived of their generation of men by the slaughter of the conflict, but retaining a great dignity and a passion for culture. Apart from inspiring Spark's most famous character, Miss Kay also inspired her intellect in other ways, giving lectures on relativity, conducting 'marvellous' scripture lessons, which led to Spark's deep knowledge and familiarity with the Bible. She shared with her pupil her sense of the poetry in the Bible, and predicted that Spark would herself be a writer.

Spark was already writing copiously in her school days and was given a prize for her poetry. She was crowned as the school's 'queen of poetry', a ceremony which nauseated her, but only Miss Kay understood why. Although it is clear that Spark was much indebted to her teacher for her early acquisition of knowledge and culture, it is also clear that her mind was very independent and developed in its own terms. Her sense of religion emerges from these reminiscences. Before she went to school, she recounts, she had a strange feeling whenever she saw the child of one of her parents' neighbours, to whom she bore an uncanny resemblance. This girl was to appear again in her later life when she was in Rhodesia, as it was then called. She was shot by her husband, an event on which Spark based her story *Bang Bang You're Dead*. Apart from this early apprehension of a mystical link in people's lives, Spark has a memory which she terms specifically a religious experience; she saw when coming from school a workman knocked down by a tram car; he ran to the side of the road, his arms stretched out before he collapsed. This image haunted her. Spark's story *The Gentile Jewess* shows how enthralled she was as a child by her mixed ancestry, a mixture which she identified in her maternal grandmother whose father was also a Jew and her mother a Gentile. This grandmother was proud of the Jewish element in her blood, and also had great sympathy for nonconformist Christian faith. She used to caricature spiritualists, re-enacting their behaviour to the excitement of her granddaughter, who was later to call on such eccentricity in *The Bachelors*. The sense of the ceremony of identity which she drew from her grandmother was to be a lasting one. At the end of *The Gentile Jewess*, probably the only purely autobiographical story she ever wrote, she explains how her ultimate Catholicism appeared to her to reconcile the different strands in her religious experience and that of the different members of her family, since 'with Roman Catholics too, it all boils down to the Almighty in the end'.

To learn from Spark's account of her early life how deeply her imagination was stirred by the people she knew is to appreciate how much she has drawn on her own experience of people for the seeds of the moral potential she develops in the characters in her novels. When I suggested to her recently that her former acquaintance, Derek Stanford, whose biography of her she finds so distastefully unreliable, might be the model for the *pisseur de copie* in *A Far Cry from Kensington*, she responded that she didn't think Stanford would actually plan to murder anybody. However, this was not a denial of my suggestion! As the development of Christina Kay in *The Prime of Miss Jean Brodie* shows, Spark has a brilliant capacity for creating plots out of the raw material to which she is so sensitive in the course of her life.

Future chapters of Spark's autobiography will shed more light on the links between her life and work. However, the basic facts are known: after she left school, she married and went with her husband to South Africa where she had a son. She returned to Britain where, in wartime, she worked for Intelligence, with a responsibility for devising broadcasts aimed at demoralizing the German war effort. After the war, Spark went into journalism and then was successful in applying for the post of secretary of the Poetry Society. She soon began to publish. In 1952 she wrote a study of John Masefield and in 1953 published a biography of Mary Shelley. She read avidly: amongst her favourite authors were Beerbohm, whose prose style she admired, Proust and Newman. Proust is mentioned in *A Far Cry from Kensington*, a novel set in the publishing world, in which Spark began to work about this time. A young writer is discussing his work with Nancy Hawkins, the main character in the novel: she is concerned that his work is too rambling and recommends that he write about 'something in particular'. The young man demands if Nancy has read Proust, thinking to cite an author who ignored this principle, but Nancy simply says of his work – 'It's about everything in particular'. This comment says much about Proust's importance for Spark. His ability to salvage the impact of the single moment perhaps suggested to Spark a way of writing in terms of the immediate, but implying with this ripple upon ripple of continuous meaning. Spark must have identified with Newman in a highly personal way; his conversion to Roman Catholicism brought to him, as to her, an essential sense of identity.

It was in fact Spark's conversion to Catholicism which was to supply the perspective so fundamental to her novels. The experience of giving over her mind to a narrative at the same time fragmentary yet adequate, was almost at one with the acceptance of an ultimate sense of things which could never be fully comprehended but which made of each particular moment an essential element of a fuller truth. Spark was now in a position to devise plots and personalities in which there was a hidden potential, often apt to rebound on the lives of those in whom it lay. She wrote of people unable to control their fortunes but reacting to this deficiency in a compellingly interesting way; sometimes with dignity and courage, sometimes with bad faith, intent on imposing a fiction and on mystifying others. There can be no doubt that the time of Spark's conversion was stressful and demanding. Yet, like Caroline, the main character in *The Comforters*, she emerged with a sense of relief; now she was free to write of life as it struck her, refusing to make facile distinctions between truth and fiction, right and wrong, but presenting her characters and the situations in which they struggle through the kaleidoscopic perspective of several responses. In this way her novels generate their own terms of reference, explicable through themselves alone and not marshalled into order by any preconceived structure.

Whilst Spark does not acknowledge a debt to so-called English Catholic writers, it is interesting to compare her approach and technique with those who immediately spring to mind: I am thinking of Greene and Waugh. Perhaps Spark's writing is closer to that of Waugh, in the sense that his Catholicism enabled him to see human motivation as self-delusory and often risible. The sardonic element of Waugh's writing has behind it a strong intimation of a tragic absence of charity in human relationships. Spark's ability to portray the ridiculousness of some of her characters revealed by their absurd pretensions is not far from the acerbic wit of Waugh.

Greene's work, on the other hand, reflects his religious sensibility in a different way; he recounts the anguish of an individual from an interior perspective. The situations in which individuals find themselves in some way bring them to confront a moral problem. They are characterized, however, not in terms of moral debate, but in responses to atmosphere, personality and emotion. Greene's characters are intrinsically inadequate, and this in itself indicates a need in them for a spiritual compensation which they search for but do not find. Spark does not write in this way; she, as narrator, is always at some distance from her characters; when she uses a first person narrative, she builds into the account an element of irony or apparently unconscious self-criticism which enables the reader to be objective. However, Spark has in common with Greene a reluctance to identify with the Roman Catholic Church in terms of its instructions and demands. Like Greene, she shows her characters in need of a higher order to demarcate, celebrate and acknowledge the challenge and tribulation of human experience. She, like Greene, is able to be critical and independent of some aspects of the Catholic Church and its practitioners. Several of her minor characters present themselves as Catholics without any idea of the experience of faith. However, as in Greene's works, the personal integrity of many of her major characters is identified with their faith, with their ability to recognize the vulnerability of others and their own need of grace.

Spark's work has attracted a good deal of critical attention in recent years. David Lodge in *The Novelist at the Crossroads* (Routledge and Kegan Paul 1971) offers a useful discussion of the narrative stance she adopts with reference to her faith. He comments that Spark's novels are distinguished by 'a highly original and effective exploitation of the convention of authorial omniscience'. Lodge discusses at length the function of narrative presentation, showing how this inevitably depends for its coherence on assumptions about the nature of providence, or its absence. He distinguishes between the Catholic writer such as Mauriac, whose authorial structure implies a perspective such as God might well have, and the writer like Graham Greene, whose characters' responses to providence are the only indication of the writer's own apprehension of the divine. Occasionally, irony in the plot implies some deeper purpose, but this is never spelt out nor developed. Muriel Spark's use of the 'convention of authorial omniscience' is equally unpretentious: 'for most of the time', writes Lodge, 'her satires are narrated from some human, limited point of view'.

Spark presents her characters and situation with mastery, never faltering in her control, and adding a dimension of wit and appreciation of irony which makes her prose sparkle. However, as Lodge says, she 'points to providence at work, but providence remains ultimately mysterious and incomprehensible, because the world is a fallen one and even the novelist cannot claim to understand it fully'. This elegant modesty does much to make her work at once unpredictable and yet endearing. Sometimes we marvel at events and reactions, and we feel that, instead of merely manipulating us, the writer is marvelling too. For Malcolm Bradbury (*Possibilities* – OUP, 1973) the essence of Spark's narrative is close to Waugh's detachment: 'Waugh', he says, 'feels free to represent the contemporary world as chaos and his characters bereft of any significant moral action'. What unity there is in Spark's narrative is, he says, aesthetic; she has no sympathy for her characters, and the wholeness of coherence of her works derives from her intelligence and her sensitivity to form as a poet. Peter Kemp's study, *Muriel Spark* (Elek, 1974), asserts that Spark's artistry is not dependent merely on aesthetic economy and tautness of plot; for him there is a rigorous moral dimension implicit in all she writes. 'The fictive organization is regarded as reflecting on a small and comparatively simple scale the vaster and more complex dispositions of divinity,' he says. There is a purpose that can be glimpsed beyond the immediate moment and, without trying to define this purpose, her writing suggests that the chaos of human activity is only an illusion; ultimately there is a sense which gives proportion to all things. Kemp points out that, although there is a satisfaction to the reader in the order, pattern and resolution of her plots, there is no place for complacency. Her themes are deeply disturbing; they cast a spotlight on the moral shortcomings of people's behaviour. 'This fiction', writes Kemp, '. . . is aimed at . . . preventing the lazy mind and torpid moral sense from lapsing into dangerous sloth . . .'

Critics have been, understandably, fascinated by the original and confident way in which Spark writes; it has been tempting to define the terms in which she works, and to read from her work some intimation of absolute points of reference, be they spiritual or aesthetic. However, such terms are elusive. I have found it rewarding to consider the perspectives and motivation of some of her characters individually. By rebuilding their understanding of their lives, their problems, their needs and their ability to confront challenges, it is possible to see how Spark portrays an experience of life to which the individual will contributes. I have studied her women characters exclusively. This is because little attention has been paid to Spark's presentation of women, although her achievement in constructing female character is unrivalled in the twentieth-century Catholic novel. Spark is not a feminist in the sense that she asserts specific rights for women, nor is she interested in decrying a society which might seek to repress women. However, she has, in several of her novels, depicted women in a search for a dignity and possession of mind which, in its own way, vindicates a woman's spiritual integrity. Waugh's women are mostly mere social satellites; Greene appears unable to present the inner consciousness of a woman – the female characters in his books are shown through the eyes of men. Muriel Spark, however, conveys an insight into the minds of her women characters which enables the reader both to identify with and to appraise their behaviour. She does not intend them to stand as exemplary figures; indeed, some are clearly flawed and wilfully contrive their own malevolent relationships. Some, though, achieve their identity through their quest for self-respect, which involves an appreciation of all that they cannot understand.

— 1 —

THE MATURE WOMAN

This heading ought perhaps to read 'the maturing woman'. The women I shall discuss in this section are portrayed in terms of their confrontations with essential problems. They all emerge stronger and more enlightened. The reader is invited to identify with them, but only to a certain extent. It is a brilliant feature of Spark's narrative technique that even in presenting a character whose responses lie at the heart of the work, she is able to include an element of irony and objectivity. Indeed, quite often, it is the very ability of the character to become self-critical that contributes the most to her development. The reader is able to observe as well as to sympathize.

The women I shall discuss in the following pages are perhaps largely identifiable with Muriel Spark herself. Certainly, the kind of challenges they face indicate the major issues of her own life. However, it is possible to see that the preoccupations which to a certain extent characterize these women are a source of creativity rather than a mere label. In their different ways, they wrestle with the terms which define their existence. They discover who they are and what they need. It is the differences in their discoveries and their needs which make each character individual, a creation in her own right. But an essential feature in the characterization of all of them is that of integrity. We are asked to see their problems as genuine, their insights as valid and their achievements as worthwhile. It is these women who on a personal level involve the reader most in the narratives which Spark devises; her wit and her flippancy are called into service to describe people and situations in their lives, but when it comes to an account of their interior experience, these skills are kept in abeyance.

Caroline Rose: *The Comforters*

The Comforters was Muriel Spark's first novel and in it she presents a character who comes to terms with the various pressures and confusions which beset the novelist. Muriel Spark makes it clear that she has no romantic illusions about the intrinsic superiority of the artist: Caroline Rose's intuitive verbalization of the situation in which she finds herself presents her with more problems than she would otherwise have, and furthermore, makes her incomprehensible to those around her. However, her appreciation of the moral dilemmas created by the circumstances around her and by her own susceptibilities gives Caroline Rose a rich maturity. She is able to develop a sense of irony about her own responses, and a recognition of her positive qualities. She also acquires a strong sense of the value of her faith and a healthy contempt for those who misrepresent it. The way in which her mind is beset by a verbal account of the thoughts and happenings in her life at first torments her. Then she finds that she can assuage and temper this experience, ultimately pacifying it by completing a novel.

Caroline is nervous and tense. At the beginning of *The Comforters* she is on retreat and finding it impossible to cope with the intrusions of one Mrs Hogg. This woman's fatuous comments about Caroline's conversion to Catholicism, her smugness and her blatantly protruding nipples irritate Caroline to the point of exasperation. On the surface, she manages to keep coolly polite, but inside she vents her private formula:

'You are damned. I condemn you to eternal flames. You are caput. You have had it, my dear.' Caroline's reactions to Mrs Hogg are shown to be more than a mere personal antipathy. Mrs Hogg's prying hypocrisy is sinister; she does her best throughout the book to undermine the integrity of other characters. Although Caroline endeavours to maintain a mood of 'sophisticated forbearance', she is overwhelmed by 'a sense of being with something abominable, not to be trusted'. The power of evil itself is in Mrs Hogg – the negation of all that is good. This idea is illustrated later in the book where it is pointed out that Mrs Hogg 'simply disappears' when alone. She has no existence except in her parasitic clinging on to those she seeks to harm.

Mrs Hogg's unpleasant interference in the lives of Caroline, her relatives and her friends, constitutes a challenge to Caroline which she has to meet with more resources than her 'private formula'. A continual dialogue with herself is her means of coping with life, and she does not fear to admit to her deficiencies. She recognizes as a weakness her 'loathing of the human flesh where the bulk outweighs the intelligence'. She is conscious of her emotional susceptibility, which she quells with acerbic irony:

> Every now and then a cynical lucidity would overtake part of her mind forcing her to comment on the fury of the other part. This was painful.

When she is alarmed by the mysterious voices she hears, she rushes to her friend the Baron for comfort. But she reproaches herself for this hasty action. She knows she has 'tough resources', and painfully she confronts her weakness in giving way to her panic. Clearly, Caroline has suffered from what she calls 'her nerves' in the past, and a vivid description of a nervous breakdown illustrates this unpleasant memory: '. . . when her brain was like a Guy Fawkes night, ideas cracking off in all directions, dark idiot-figures jumping around a fiery junk heap in the centre.' However, the course of the novel, alongside the amusing and glittering account of her friend's grandmother's smuggling gang, shows how Caroline develops. She recognizes her resources, and methodically teaches herself to cope with her wilder reactions, subduing these to her faith.

Laurence, Caroline's former lover, with whom she retains a close friendship, acts as a foil to Caroline in the narrative. He is bright, curious and lively, but has no capacity for reflection and was not 'a wonderer'. His wise grandmother, Louisa, recognizes this, but indulges him since her affection for him is so great, even though his inquisitiveness is a threat to her smuggling ring. Caroline loves Laurence, but is fully conscious of his relative superficiality. She is impatient with his desire to try to record the mysterious voices she hears, knowing herself that they 'might have another sort of existence and still be real'. She resents his attempt to find a 'technological solution' to everything. Nevertheless, she admits to herself that she tolerates in Laurence things she would be unable to bear in others. 'And she was aware of the irrationality and prejudice of all these feelings without being able to stop feeling them.'

Caroline has a sense of mystery, and finds a mystery in herself. She is humble in her willingness to acquiesce before her experience but courageous in her efforts to establish a moral focal point in it. A central theme of the narrative is the occurrence of the voices and typing which Caroline hears when alone in her flat. This experience is bewildering to her. It is not diminished nor contained by explanations offered her by her friends ('the comforters'). She refuses to agree that she is suffering a mental breakdown, knowing that the onset of the voices is quite different from her 'Guy Fawkes night' experience of the past. Far from explosions and confusions, this time her thoughts are all assembled and verbalized in a most organized way. Then she realizes, in discussing the experience with her priest, that the voices suggest the formation of a novel in which she and her acquaintances all play a rôle. The writer, she decides, 'lives in a different dimension from ours'. The intrusion of the voices, the imposition of a verbalization of her experience, have brought to Caroline a 'new form of suffering' which she has to accept. She does so, with a resignation towards the incomprehensibility of this experience in the minds of others and initially in her own mind.

> For my own experiences however I don't demand anyone's belief. You may call them delusions, for all I care. I have merely registered my findings.

She declares to Laurence that it would be a shirking of spiritual responsibility to deny what is happening to her: 'From the Catholic point of view, the chief danger about a conviction is the attempt to deny it.'

The disturbing experience of the intrusive voices presents a challenge to Caroline. She manages to control her initial panic, and faces them as a fact, as painful as her faith, she says. Once she has conceded that the voices and typing indicate a novel under way, she carefully endeavours to establish her relationship with the 'unknown writer'. She is suspicious, and at one point has 'a shapeless idea that Mrs Hogg was in league with her invisible persecutors'. In other words, she feels that the intrusion of the novel into her thoughts might be evil. She resists when the voices anticipate her actions. She tries her best to travel by train to Cornwall, once the voices have said that she and Laurence would take the car. But, discovering that it was a holy day of obligation, she realizes she must miss the train in order to go to mass. At this point, she gives in, recognizing the inclusion of her own moral needs in the novel's structure. She is determined not to allow herself to be governed by 'some unknown, possibly sinister being'. She declares that she intends to subject it to reason. 'I happen to be a Christian', she asserts, and it is clear that the point of reference provided by her faith is going to decide the perspective by which she comes to terms with the voices. One criterion Caroline establishes is that she wants the novel to have a dimension other than the 'conveniently slick plot'. She wants to 'stand aside, and see if the novel has any real form'. Reality means to Caroline inclusion of the spiritual dimension. Ultimately, she hastens to complete the novel, feeling that the narrative would be clear when she was outside it.

The evidence of her sanity would be in the book itself, she states. There are many implications here about the novelist's relationship with her work. Caroline wishes to learn from her experience, but she does not want her novelist's wiles to organize and create it into a 'slick plot'. Nor does she wish to be predestined by the novelist's anticipation of what would 'fit'. Although these matters are not analysed in *The Comforters*, it is clear that they constitute a major preoccupation of Muriel Spark. It is also implicit that they are resolved for Caroline, thanks to her acquiescence before the permanent values of her faith, and her confidence in her intelligence. Muriel Spark is willing to accept the arbitrariness of personal perceptions, and genuinely poses the question: 'Is the world a lunatic asylum, then? Are we all courteous maniacs, discreetly making allowances for everyone else's derangement?' The irony resulting from the differences in personal motive and situation constitutes an important element in the fabric of Muriel Spark's writing in this book. But the central character is able to perceive herself with honesty, since she is aware of the truth quoted by her lapsed Catholic friend, Laurence: 'Let nothing disturb thee, nothing afright thee, all things are passing, God never changeth.'

Caroline Rose's struggle to respond to and yet control her own mental activity is the principal theme of this book. It is this struggle, sometimes incomprehensible and lonely, which characterizes her. It distances her from other people in the book, since none of them recognizes nor understands her difficulties. But since their very nature is ultimately to decide her identity as a writer, it is essential that she confront them on her own. The context of Laurence's grandmother's smuggling ring, the odd characters who are involved with one another in a sinister but amusing way, all contribute to suggest how arbitrary and circumstantial are the events of life. But the solidity of the identity of these people is not questioned; only the predatory hypocritical Mrs Hogg is denied any moral substance. Just as Caroline in an emotive moment once condemns her to eternal flames, she is shown to have no full existence at all. Caroline's existence on the other hand is even fuller than that of the other characters, although they are involved in their smuggling and in their relationships with one another. Her identity as a writer makes her life more troublesome but ultimately richer.

The reader gets to know Caroline through an account of the way her mind works. However, various other personal qualities are indicated through her relationship with others. We see that she is fiercely independent. Although she is fond of Laurence it is obvious that she has more respect for her own judgement than for his. She is ready to impose celibacy on them both as an act of submission to her newly found faith. But she still needs and values his affection and his companionship. She is fearful of acquiring an image in her own mind of becoming some kind of nervous wreck. Her triumph is that she accepts her mental experience in all its obscurity and confusion, and sees in it a source of response to the arbitrariness of the world and to one implicit truth. From this source of response emerges her novel and the main theme of *The Comforters*.

January Marlow: *Robinson*

Muriel Spark's second novel *Robinson* has been seen as a symbolic mental landscape, as a portrait of a personal psychological experience – quite possibly, that of the author. However, such an interpretation does not acknowledge the full coherence of the book. In terms of plot alone – tension, mystery, surprise – the story has considerable momentum. Paradoxically, the rich psychological dimension of the book is not an interior perspective; it is through the interrelation of the personalities that the moral implications of their attitudes and behaviour become clear.

January Marlow is the central character of the book, which is recounted in the first person. All that happens is seen in terms of her reactions. The narrative assumes a conversational familiarity with the reader, although this does not mean that we are not in a position to see January objectively. She is sufficiently honest with herself to record discrepancies in her own outlook, and we see incongruities and contradictions in her. However her very deficiencies make us – and her – more aware of the tensions and challenges to which she is submitted during her stay on Robinson. The struggle she endures to sustain her integrity is one in which self-knowledge is the surest safeguard.

January is the only woman on the island Robinson after a plane crash. She is left on the island with two male survivors, Robinson – the only inhabitant of the island – and his adopted child. The trauma of the crash has a profound effect on her, but, as the days go by, she is able to adjust. Intent on keeping her mind as clear as possible, she seeks to conserve her dignity in a situation which could threaten it.

The relationships which develop amongst the oddly assorted group of people on the island provide the catalyst for their identities. January, from the beginning, feels both defensive towards and intrigued by the others. Having recovered from the initial shock of the crash and its immediate aftermath, she realizes how involved she is becoming with their personalities. 'I . . . was irritated by this curiosity of mine which did so indicate that these people were becoming part of my world.' She resents what she considers to be unwarranted intrusions into her mind. In the course of her reflections on her irritation, she states how important it is to her to be in 'control' of her relationships. She likes to be 'in a position to choose'.

However, her instinctive responses get the better of her, and she becomes increasingly conscious of the emotive effect her companions have on her. Jimmy, the Dutchman who turns out to be a relative of Robinson, she finds endearing. His appeal lies largely in his eccentric command of English, mostly culled from seventeenth-century texts lent to him by a Swiss uncle. This odd diction makes his personality both naive and strangely sophisticated. Although Tom Wells, the other stranded male passenger, insinuates that January is physically attracted to Jimmy, she is very conscious that her feelings towards him are quite different from what Tom Wells imagines: 'Jimmy appealed to a quality in my mind which I considered to be the most advanced I possessed; and which was also slightly masculine.'

This 'masculine' quality in fact appears throughout the book; January is determined to be regarded by her companions as an equal, and she strongly resents any suggestion that her sex incapacitates her either mentally or physically. Jimmy's straightforward friendship appeals to her. He is willing to share his ideas with her, and they chat amicably about the events of their life on the island. As well as providing January with much entertainment, Jimmy is also a great help in her efforts to maintain her dignity.

When January sticks together the pages of Tom Wells' torn magazine, Tom thanks her in a way she finds offensive:

'That's sweet of you, honey,' said Wells.
    'Is not to call Miss January honey,' said Jimmy, 'as if she was a trumpet . . . and any –'
    'You mean strumpet,' I said.
    'Strumpet,' said Jimmy, 'and any indignities vented upon this lady, I black your eye fullsore.'

January's irritation with Tom Wells has many causes. She resents his clumsy passes. When she is sent to take soup to him as he recovers from injuries sustained in the crash, he calls her a 'nice piece of homework', and she deliberately drops the soup on him. His insensitivity annoys her. Robinson puts some music on the record player and Tom Wells crassly talks through it. His brash conceit is made even more unbearable by the ineptitude of his remarks: 'It's unnatural living like this alone with Nature,' he would say, 'but we're lucky to be alive.' January's dislike of Tom, however, lies at a level deeper than the cerebral. She admits as much to herself. When Robinson advises Tom to join them in playing chess, saying it is good for the mind, Tom retorts that Robinson had no right to say what was good for *his* mind. January thinks this 'reasonable enough', but finds that she is not sympathetic to Tom because she 'just doesn't like him'.

January finds Tom Wells nauseating, for his clumsy flirtatiousness, for his crassness, for his stupidity. But there is something more sinister about him. His trade in lucky charms grates on January's religious sensibility. Although she feels contemptuous of the tales he weaves about 'Ethel of the Well', nonetheless, it is clear that there is some basic fundamental opposition in Tom's and January's understanding of the metaphysical. When Tom claims that one of his charms had brought him the luck to be saved from the accident, January remarks: 'It would have been luckier if there had been no accident'. When, later in the book, Tom Wells tries to blackmail January and Jimmy into signing a false account of Robinson's disappearance so that none of them is blamed for his murder, the depth of the antagonism between January and Wells sharpens dramatically. He has taken her diary in which there is a full account of the events on the island, and she retrieves it, seeking to hide it underground in the myriad tunnels which run beneath the island.

Wells pursues her with a knife; she eludes him and eventually collapses exhausted on the soaking ground. The fact that Robinson is not dead, and that consequently January's fears that Tom might be the murderer prove unfounded, in no way invalidates the intensity of their mutual dislike. Wells has no respect for January as a woman, he is egocentric, and worst of all seeks power over others with his spurious charms. January senses the fraudulence in him. On the island, the fascination of his lucky charms only works on the boy Miguel, but it later emerges that in England there is a network of people allured, deceived and exploited by his superstitious trade.

January Marlow: *Robinson*

It is through her relationship with Robinson that January learns most, although he is deliberately remote and clearly intends to have no close contact with any of his unexpected visitors. She realizes soon after their arrival that he does not respond to what she terms 'the feminine element in women', but decides that this does not suggest any homosexuality in him; it is more that he is 'like a priest'. In many ways, January is angered by Robinson's self-sufficiency. When she takes a look at his bookshelf and notices many uncut first editions, she is contemptuous of him for bringing such esoteric items on to the island. She is also irritated by his apparent refusal to cultivate the ground on the island, eating out of tins, instead of growing a kitchen garden. Nevertheless, she cannot help identifying with him in certain ways. She admits to herself that she 'felt rather sorry for Robinson', since his seclusion was so suddenly threatened by their arrival. When they do discuss together, they are sparring partners, rather than friends. She regards him as patronizing. His very supervision of the island incites some resentment in her, as if, in some way, he threatened her independence. It is only after Robinson's disappearance that January comes to realize how much she was drawn to him. She then thinks seriously about the way in which Robinson had come to their aid, not only physically, but in the way he had welcomed them into his home. Her most pleasant hours on the island had been spent listening to Robinson telling stories and legends of the place. She was, additionally, fascinated by his religious convictions. He was even more angered than she by Tom Wells' superstitious charms and, although at first intensely annoyed when he removed her rosary beads, she understands that he is 'constitutionally afraid of any material manifestation of grace'. Nosing around his private papers, she discovers how ardently he had written against the Marian cult in the Church. He had trained initially to be a priest, and after his disappearance she finds that she feels towards him very much as to a priest: when she thinks of him she is 'overwhelmed by cousinly love'. His presumed death shows her both an heroic character, and a pre-Christian victim of expiation. This 'death' has a very marked effect on her; she no longer feels 'creepy' about using objects belonging to the dead passengers which had been salvaged from the plane; this was one superstition which Robinson's influence had ultimately rid her of. Most importantly, she feels differently towards Tom and even Jimmy. She sees them as strangers; even Jimmy has lost his charm for her. They are 'on the same island, but in different worlds'. It is very clear that the residual effect of the image left by Robinson's character has a strong spiritual influence on January. When he returns and she discovers that his death has been faked, she is at first very angry. She thinks that his behaviour has been the result of a personal whim with no consideration of the effect it would have on others. She explains her annoyance: 'I chucked the antinomian pose when I was twenty. There's no such thing as a private morality.' However, her ultimate reflection on Robinson is one of gratitude. 'But really, after all, it was his island, and he probably had, at the start, saved our lives.'

The overall impact of the book gives the impression that Robinson had saved more than their lives; he had saved their sanity. After his disappearance, they change. Tom Wells and January are sick with loathing for one another; at one point he looks close to killing her. Jimmy holds no interest for January any more; she despises his weakness in agreeing to sign the fraudulent statement that Tom Wells has composed. All the characters are estranged from one another. Robinson was the civilizing element on the island, which, as January observes, arouses strong pagan forces. Her perceptions, as she says, were touched by a pre-ancestral quality, a primitive blood force. She feels strangely drawn to worship the moon. Although she is throughout her ordeal conscious of her 'professional independence', her 'pride', her identity as a writer, her dignity as a woman, it is basically her awareness of a fundamental truth in all things which sustains her, and this is a truth to which Robinson is equally acquiescent. When Wells and Jimmy agree to fabricate the circumstances of Robinson's disappearance,

January does everything to save her diary in which there is an accurate account. Without her hold on truth and Robinson's integrity, the events on the island would have degenerated into a pagan amorality and mutual exploitation.

After the rescue, January admits, reminiscing over espresso coffee or walking down the King's Road, Chelsea, that when she remembers the island, immediately 'all things are possible'. It is a tribute to her self-knowledge and appreciation of good, that she has survived the terrible threats of infinite possibility, and finds now in this a cause for celebration.

January's acknowledgement of her vulnerability whilst on the island, her realization of her many changes of mood, her acceptance of the intensity of her emotional reactions contribute to the development of this vital self knowledge. Far from being mere weaknesses, these manifestations of her humanity become a source of strength. They make her appreciate her fundamental need of a grasp on truth.

January Marlow is fiercely independent. She resents Tom Wells' flirtatiousness, which she regards as insulting. Although she admits to missing her make-up on the island, her principal consciousness of her femininity is defensive. She acknowledges that there is a strong streak of masculinity in her, and this makes her want to be treated as an equal. Her positive response to Jimmy in the early stages of the book is based on a sense of affection and companionship. Her increasing involvement with Robinson is more complex; she identifies spiritually with him and respects him for his combination of generosity and guardedness. It is her understanding of Robinson that helps her develop. Instead of resorting to an air of offended dignity and petulance, which was even then a dated form of asserting femininity, she strives to build her thoughts on the one valuable relationship she has discovered. The intense 'cousinly love' she feels for Robinson has a maturing effect on her. He is as protective and as enlightening as a priest. There are few references in the book to a need of an orthodox religious structure; January misses her make-up more than hearing mass. On the other hand, a need of

moral priorities emerges very strongly. The tensions which result
from the encounter of different personalities on the island are
magnified as a result of their isolation. As a consequence of the
threat of disintegration of all civilized attitudes, January comes to
appreciate the strength of the values which Robinson has, in his
solitary existence, striven to nurture. It is through this realization
that she enlarges her own spiritual horizon and is ready to take
on the terrible truth that all things are possible.

Barbara Vaughan: *The Mandelbaum Gate*

Barbara Vaughan is a character of contrasts. These contrasts
emphasize the duality of her ancestry: Jew and Gentile. She
feels that 'the essential thing about her remained unspoken,
uncharacterized and unlocated'. The search Barbara pursues
to establish her identity is the subject of this book. The story
is ostensibly that of her pilgrimage to the Holy Land, where,
despite being a Catholic, her Jewish ancestry makes it dangerous
for her to travel beyond the frontiers of Israel into Jordan where
many of the holy sites are situated. With the help of Freddy
Hamilton, the effete, well-meaning British consul, and some
of his Arab friends, she is able to cross secretly into Jordan
and continue her pilgrimage, disguised as an Arab servant. This
somewhat unlikely story comprises, however, only one level of
the experience which Barbara must face. On a deeper, spiritual
and psychological level, she must find herself.

A detailed account is given of Barbara's childhood, in the
course of which she was already very conscious of the disparity
between her Jewish mother's family and that of her English
father. She has vivid memories of eating cucumber sandwiches
on the lawn of her Vaughan grandmother, a strapping tennis
player, radiant with energy; she recalls hearing the beech leaves
'like papers being shuffled into order' at the end of an English

afternoon 'with its fugitive sorrow'. Although the English family was so discreet and unobtrusive, an element of this life had touched Barbara deeply: 'the air was elusively threaded with the evidence of unseen hyacinths', and 'the lawn lay as beautiful as eternity' – these were perceptions with which her mind responded to the contained elegance of her English relations and which suggest the spiritual value she found in them. The contrast between this life and her subsequent visit to her Jewish family at Golders Green brings out clearly the difference both in ethos and personality of the two halves of her parentage. She was fascinated by the Passover commemoration: the items on the side table, the eggs, the cake, the paschal lamb. But most of all she recalls the unleavened bread:

> it was not actually the same wafery substance here on the table at Golders Green, that had been baked by the Israelites on the first passover night and yet in a mysterious sense it was: 'This is the bread which our fathers ate . . .'

Barbara's future conversion to Catholicism is already being nurtured by her understanding of the Jewish ceremony.

Now Barbara is an adult, her character appears formed and her life organized. On the surface, Barbara has managed to develop a formal, almost prim personality. She is an English teacher in a private school, the close friend of another teacher, Miss Rickward. However, although to the world 'a settled spinster of thirty-seven' she has found a lover who has changed her life. The account given of Barbara's love affair with Harry, a shy, unpretentious archaeologist, shows how this relationship marks the beginning of her self-discovery. Her image as an English spinster she now feels to be a disguise. Harry Clegg acts as a catalyst to bring out something essential in her personality which hitherto had been entirely separate from the image she presented to the world. Her love for Harry was a sensational discovery: 'She felt herself to be in love with Harry Clegg in an entirely exclusive form as yet unrealized in human experience.'

Simultaneously, her sexuality rises to the surface; she feels herself to be blessed by sex, and attributes this spontaneous enjoyment to her Jewish blood. Her love for Harry gives her a sense of identity which quite transcends the spinsterish school teacher she had been before.

There is, however, a complication in their relationship, which brings into conflict Barbara's need of Harry and her need of the Church. Little is said about the time of her conversion; it appears to have developed naturally from her spiritual sensibility, which grew in different ways, in the alternate climates of her childhood. Harry is married and, although he is determined to seek an annulment, it is not certain that this will be possible. Barbara therefore has a problem which overshadows her newfound happiness and her liberated identity. She has no doubts of her desire to marry, but she is most reluctant to be severed from the Church. One thing she perceives very clearly; she cannot repent of love. This realization is not a rejection of the Church's teaching; on the contrary, it is shown as an acknowledgement of a profound element of faith.

Her departure to Israel coincides with Harry's archaeological work around the Dead Sea. Over this period, separated from him geographically, by the problems which have arisen about their relationship and reluctant to sleep with him again until these have been resolved, Barbara is aware of her isolation. It is however a fertile time in which her mind is hard at work, questioning herself about who she is. She hopes that her pilgrimage will throw light on this.

Much information is given about Barbara's life retrospectively, but the crux of the book is the revelation she derives from her time in Israel and Jordan. Until her affair with Harry Clegg, she has lived as an English school mistress, sober and subdued. The emancipation of her passionate personality begins when she meets Harry and then, once in Israel, is to continue. Once involved with Harry, she realizes that her 'self-image is at variance with the image she presented to the world'. In Israel, the self-image begins to break through. We learn this through the reactions of the consul, Freddy. When he first meets her, he is delighted to find 'a pleasant English spinster'. But then, when he passes a mild comment on how extreme the Church's insistence on annulment of Harry's marriage appears to him, he is bewildered by Barbara's response. Virulently, she quotes from the Apocalypse, condemning all that is mediocre: 'Being what thou art, neither cold nor hot I will vomit thee out of my mouth.' He finds her words incomprehensible, her voice cold and terrifying. Elsewhere, he refers to her as a 'frail, dark, merry woman, fearfully indiscreet'. The veneer of prim convention no longer conceals Barbara. She finds that she resents the assumptions about her identity as a spinster which have hitherto rendered her bland and uninteresting: 'What right have they to take me at my face value? Every spinster should be assumed guilty before she is assumed innocent.'

The rejection of the 'lukewarm' in the piece of Scripture that Barbara so angrily quoted at Freddy has begun to characterize her outlook. Her love for Harry is one essential element she has discovered in her life. Another is her faith, equally passionate and equally illuminating. Just as her relationship with Harry revealed to her a new dimension in her experience, so her faith gives her a sense of ultimate value. We are told elsewhere in the narrative that Barbara detests ideologies. All that is arid, objective, bureaucratic, coldly analytical is to her anathema. This distinction is nowhere more apparent than when Barbara attends the trial of Adolf Eichmann, currently taking place in Jerusalem. The mechanical way in which Eichmann answers the questions put to him strikes her as 'the meticulous, undiscriminating reflex of a computer machine'. She finds the most terrible incongruity between the 'dead, mechanical tick' with which Eichmann speaks and the living horror of his subject: the massacre. Barbara reels at the disparity between the spiritual outrage and the bureaucratic mechanism of the court room, she turns to the idea of her pilgrimage, which alone gives her a sense of truth and purpose.

Barbara's faith is precious to her; it provides the only valid point of reference she knows. Freddy had unconsciously recognized this: '(she) was the sort of person who somehow induced one to think in terms of religion, if one thought about her at all.' As Barbara disappears over the border to Jordan, we are very conscious that she, as a Jew, is in danger although she makes light of it herself. Her time in the shelter of the hermit's hut on the Potter's Field, where Judas was reputed to have sold Christ's life, forms a central point in the book. The threat to her as she makes her pilgrimage under the heavy cover of her peasant wrapping is not merely the fun of an illicit adventure, as it seemed at the beginning. Barbara is unwell, and, as she looks upon the stone slab, reputedly the Holy Sepulchre, she longs only to lie on it and for the sleep of death. Barbara's physical and emotional vulnerability are very apparent at this point. Although at other moments in the narrative we are told of a highly conscious, intellectual appraisal of events going on in her mind, she is now at the mercy of forces beyond her. While she is in this condition, indebted only to her faith to tell her why she is where she is, the perspective of the religious dimension is presented through the sermon of a young 'renegade' priest, who, without permission, decides to address a few words to the party of Catholic pilgrims he is accompanying. His views strike nearby friars as extremely unorthodox. However, in terms of Spark's narrative, they are most meaningful. The priest discounts the gaudy commercialism that surrounds the shrines. Similarly, he discounts the superstitious attitude of some pilgrims who rush around in an effort to touch every shrine, like a child leaping the cracks in the pavement. The individual sense of piety, the aesthetic responses of the pilgrims were unimportant; they were arbitrary. What mattered was their disposition and what mattered about Jerusalem was the spiritual city that is involved eternally with the historical one; the place not only of Christ's death, but of his resurrection.

Barbara hardly listens to the sermon; her fever makes her miserable and unresponsive. To her the sermon is just 'a sanctimonious voice pounding upon her physical distress'. However, the priest's thoughts illuminate for the reader the motive of Barbara's pilgrimage in a way of which not even she herself is conscious. He says that to make a pilgrimage is an instinct of humankind; an act of devotion which, like a work of art, has meaning enough in itself. Faith alone illuminates truth; everything beyond what may be perceived through faith, it is better to doubt. 'But in whatever touches the human spirit, it is better to believe everything than nothing.'

Barbara does not hear these words, but her own thoughts described in the course of the narrative, complement them. Although, as we learn early on, she is aware of her honest, analytical intelligence, she does not look to this alone to establish meaning in her life. She is equally aware of her 'beautiful, dangerous gift of faith'. It is this faith which has prompted her pilgrimage, just as the priest indicates. It is also her faith that gives her the ability to accept her own limitations. She knows that she cannot, unaided, find satisfaction either in immediate circumstances or in her own responses; she has a kind of 'divine discontent':

> my mind is impatient to escape from its constitution and reach its point somewhere else. In the meantime, what is to be borne is to be praised. In the meantime, memory circulates like the bloodstream. May mine circulate well, may it bring dead facts to life, may it bring health to whatever is to be borne.

She acknowledges that she has a spiritual responsibility to try and identify the good and the true, and to discover lasting value in her own experience. This is why she turns to the concept of her pilgrimage, when she is so appalled by the mechanical inhumanity of Adolf Eichmann. There are polarities in her own life, and it is very much part of her pilgrimage to establish these. She does not look to her own ability to analyse in order to solve problems. Her faith tells her that there is an answer, and this very conviction lends questions 'a still beauty'. She realizes too that actions are prompted by 'a helpless complexity of motives'.

What is important is that these should harmonize. As we hear of Barbara's thoughts, we understand that through her faith she is coming to terms with the ignorance and confusion of the human condition, trusting that there are absolute values, and patiently endeavouring to find her identity within them. She concludes with the words of Jehovah: 'I am who I am.'

Finally, it is possible for Harry and Barbara to marry. The jealous Miss Rickward has photocopied Harry's birth certificate, showing both that he is illegitimate and that his mother was a Catholic. Wrongly, she has assumed that these facts will prove sufficiently damaging to make marriage between Barbara and Harry totally unacceptable. But, paradoxically, they invalidate Harry's previous marriage, and thus he and Barbara are free. This unexpected turn of events resolves the story line, and, we are told, Barbara and Harry live 'fairly happily' ever after and fuss terribly over their only child, a daughter. The offhand way in which this information is imparted indicates that the relationship between Harry and Barbara has not been of essential importance to the narrative except in a circumstantial way. We have hardly seen them with each other, and are told that their letters read like essays in theology. The important relationship is that of Barbara with herself.

In a sense this is resolved through her ability to encounter herself and to acknowledge different factors in her personality which she has hitherto kept suppressed. The reader too is asked to reconcile her deep faith, her sober thoughts and her passionate emotions. Her physical attack on Ruth Gardnor, at whom she throws a vase and a clock, is hard to assimilate, even though Barbara is ill and has been incarcerated with Ruth for some days. One assumes that this aggression is Barbara's extreme reaction to the constantly repeated political convictions of her companion. Even so it seems unlikely and surprisingly, Barbara never reflects on this uncontrolled breakout. However, we are perhaps meant to understand that the intensity of Barbara's behaviour on occasion shows how much she needs her faith. She admits that she is prepared to wed Harry Clegg even without the sanction of the Church, but she says it is the 'keeping it up' she was afraid of, meaning keeping up the courage to stay out of the Church. She realized it would have been a risk to her marriage as she would have found no peace of mind. 'Either the whole of life is unified under God, or it falls apart,' she thinks. It is this need for reconciliation of all the elements within her mind which prompts her pilgrimage.

Barbara finds that her experiences in Israel and Jordan have helped her to see her life in perspective. The horror of the Eichmann case lay in the abyss it implied; a glimpse of the unfathomable depths of inhumanity, which made the mind panic. As Barbara realizes, one has to look for a reality to which to cling. She finds this in her faith, and in her decision to get married. She acknowledges the strength of her intellect, but her faith gives her the humility to value this at its true worth: essentially intellectual analysis is negative:

We must all think in vague terms: with God all things are possible: because the only possibilities we ever seem able to envisage in a precise manner are disastrous events.

This realization gives her an inner calm, transcending her troubled surroundings, soothing her restless intellect. Having discovered her spiritual self, she knows who she is.

Barbara is characterized in terms of her passionate emotional inner life which is so intense that sometimes even she does not understand it. We see that she has a considerable impact on others because of this intensity. We are reminded often in the course of the narrative that she is aware of her intellectual ability. *The Mandelbaum Gate*, however, recounts a period in her life when these are no longer in control and she is in the power of her susceptibility to passionate response. Although her relationship with Harry Clegg is pivotal in the plot, it is not central in describing Barbara's experience. What really matters is her faith which she finds increasingly gives her a new identity. When she is in Jordan she experiences a longing for death on reaching the Holy Sepulchre. Her impatience with the politics of Ruth Gardnor, with whom she has to stay, even leads her to violence.

The passionate elements in Barbara's character are left deliberately uncircumscribed. They are a mystery and can be bridled by faith alone. She has discovered through her pilgrimage that she could not renounce her faith to marry Clegg. But through force of circumstances and the irony of her blundering schoolmistress friend, it becomes possible for the marriage to take place. It is however implicit in the narrative that however much happiness this marriage brought Barbara, it would never provide her with the same scope as her faith.

Fleur Talbot: *Loitering with Intent*

Loitering with Intent is Muriel Spark's second novel about a writer. It is narrated in the first person, and the character of the narrator, Fleur Talbot, has positive qualities which enliven her account and endear her to her readers. Her style is relaxed and chatty, her love of life evident and above all, she is exuberant about writing. Her awareness of her identity as a writer dynamizes the narrative; it gives a sharp focus to her experience which she is able to evaluate clearly with her writer's mind. Fleur has powers of perception which contribute to the quality both of her craft and of her life. Her creative gift does not set her apart from others; she is highly involved with her friends and with people she meets in the course of her work as secretary to Sir Quentin Oliver. Indeed, it is through her encounters with others that the story evolves. It evolves not in terms of events and circumstance, but of moral confrontation from which values emerge, vindicating Fleur and her creativity.

Fleur Talbot: *Loitering with Intent*

The novel opens with Fleur sitting on a gravestone writing a poem. She has no job, her rent is overdue, but she is relaxed and happy. Already one is aware of an inner momentum which is of far greater importance than pressures from the outside world. The novelist in her is able to create a positive resource from every aspect of her experience; she is 'fascinated by the swinishness' of her landlord, who wishes her to move into a more expensive room, and with his wife who steps in and out condescendingly, her nails polished and her hair glossy black. One of Fleur's strongest characteristics as a novelist is her thirst for the detail of other people's personalities; their mannerisms, their predictable little phrases, the way they dress, and, above all, their assumptions. Before the book is much under way, Fleur makes a statement about her delight in the amazing variety and richness in other people's characters:

In fact I was aware of a *demon* inside me that rejoiced in seeing people as they were, and not only that, but more than ever as they were, and more and more.

Fleur finds a job, and it is around the work she is offered that the plot revolves. Sir Quentin Oliver has what he calls an Autobiographical Association, a collection of people who have agreed to write their autobiographies under his auspices. Fleur is to correct the syntax, generally improve the presentation of their labours, under strict secrecy. She is fascinated by the strange set-up. Although none of the writers had got beyond the first chapter of their autobiographies, Fleur is able to identify the 'nostalgia, paranoia, and craving for a likeable image' which they all have in common. She discerns the lack of inner standards of these people, realizing that they are out of control of the various wisps of recollection they offer in their accounts. Initially nauseated by these, Fleur sets to work making them 'expertly worse'. She invents anecdotes which make them more readable and when presented with her alterations the members of the Association do not object at all. The initial fun of elaborating on these 'dreary

41

biographies' wears off and Fleur is relieved when Sir Quentin decides to take them off her hands. The truth is that he has got to the point he was waiting for; the members, stimulated by Fleur's lively alterations but above all by Sir Quentin's insistence that they be governed by 'complete frankness', have begun to divulge details of their amorous experiences. Sir Quentin tells Fleur that there is now an important moral question involved. He comments that the writers do not appear to have a sufficiently strong sense of guilt. Fleur is now glad to be told that she would no longer play any part in the composition of the memoirs. From the beginning, she has been suspicious of Sir Quentin's desire to have the autobiographies written, and particularly of the power he is acquiring over the members of the group. She later learns that he has been encouraging them to take dexedrine, which decreases the appetite and lowers the morale. One member commits suicide as a result.

Fleur decides ultimately that Sir Quentin is evil. When she first started to work for him, she was intrigued. His list and description of the members of his group she saw as a kind of poem; his choice of detail, his odd vocabulary enchanted her; she was impressed by the amount of 'religious energy' that had gone into its composition. She rejoices in it because it was assembled energetically but unconsciously; the style is essentially Sir Quentin's own. However, this response to the poetic qualities of Sir Quentin's list is simply her writer's understanding of the impact of words assembled spontaneously. When she observes Sir Quentin's behaviour amongst the members of his group, the hold he has over them, the dwindling of their resistance to him, she has a great sense of his tyranny and power of exploitation.

The tale of Sir Quentin's sinister enterprise and the odd personalities involved in it makes lively reading and provides a stimulating foil for Fleur's responsive qualities. However, the situation is more complex than the basic features of the story suggest. Fleur participates in the Association's activities, initially through making somewhat facetious additions to their manuscripts. But later she discovers that her involvement with them is more subtle and surprising. She is currently completing her first novel, *Warrender Chase*, and the resemblances between the characters in her book and those she encounters through the Association strike her increasingly. She is bemused and intrigued by this. She reads some sections from her novel to her ex-lover's wife, Dottie, a casual friend of hers, and whom she introduces to the Association. Dottie recounts to Sir Quentin the disturbing similarities between Fleur's typescript and his life. Between them they contrive to steal the novel.

The story of this theft and the way in which Fleur sets about retrieving her beloved work is entertaining and stimulates the pace of the narrative. But this development is not merely on the level of a detective story. Fleur's novel would appear to possess some kind of power which has both alarmed and magnetized Sir Quentin. Fleur catches sight of her typescript in one of the drawers in his office. She realizes in the same moment that Sir Quentin is actually using some of the text as he speaks. He accuses her of having 'delusions of grandeur', a phrase drawn directly from her book. The similarities between her composition and real life events increase until Sir Quentin, exactly like his parallel character in her book, is killed in a car crash.

Both Dottie and Sir Quentin accuse Fleur of being evil. Dottie tells her reprovingly that she is 'out of her element in this world'. Fleur herself is puzzled by what appears to be an element of prophecy in her writing. But she is happy to 'wonder everything'; it is part of her faith. What stands out clearly to the reader is Fleur's deep capacity for moral perception, and this is linked strongly with the theme of autobiographical writing. Sir Quentin's captive members are told to write the stories of their lives so that he can insinuate himself into their minds and discover their weaknesses, ultimately to establish power over them. It is amusing to Fleur that, although they are flattered, as Sir Quentin intends, by his assurance of the importance of their autobiographical accounts, they have no idea how to write them, nor what to write. Fleur, on the other hand, is now in fact herself writing a 'section of her autobiography' as she tells the tale of her encounter with Sir Quentin. It is clear that she knows herself, can evaluate her abilities and her shortcomings and that she has an instinctive sense of proportion with which to present the events and personalities which contribute to her narrative.

The polarities of authentic and inauthentic writing about one's own life are established in *Loitering with Intent* through reference to the skimpy and inadequate efforts of Sir Quentin's coterie, and to the contrasting elegance and import of Newman's *Apologia* and the *Life* of Benvenuto Cellini. Fleur quotes Cellini lovingly, identifying his 'love affair with his art' with her own vital passion. Like Cellini, she finds momentum in the beauty and complexity of her experience and 'goes on her way rejoicing'. Newman she admires for his ability to present his life in terms of his faith. She brings the *Apologia* to the attention of the Autobiographical Association early in her days of working with Sir Quentin. She feels particularly that Newman might help a woman called Maisie, crippled by polio, who thinks exclusively in abstract terms, and on a personal level is bitterly humbled by her disability. Fleur thinks that 'the sublime pages' of Newman's autobiography would tether her to the 'sweet world of living people'. However, Maisie only extracts the concept of an exclusive 'I-and-thou' relationship with God, which irritates Fleur. Worse still, Fleur finds that Sir Quentin is becoming a distorted reflection of Newman; having encountered Newman through Fleur, he justifies himself in terms of his life.

'You are a fiend,' says Sir Quentin, 'your enthusiasm for John Henry Newman was pure hypocrisy. Did he not form under his influence a circle of devoted spiritual followers? Am I not entitled to do the same?'

It is clear to the reader that other characters in this book perceive themselves and one another from a point of view quite different from Fleur's. Dottie and Sir Quentin accuse Fleur of being evil, of being 'harsh'. They are alarmed by her because her insight unnerves them. When Fleur discovers the similarities between her novel and Sir Quentin's entourage, she is somewhat unnerved herself. But overwhelmingly, this strange fact gives her pleasure; the occurrence of the same situation and relationships in real life confirms her power of intuitive creation. There is a strong link throughout *Loitering with Intent* between Fleur's gifts as a writer, her integrity and her faith.

The disparity between Fleur's perceptions and those of Dottie, the 'English rose', suggests the enlightenment of Fleur's outlook, and the muddle of Dottie's mind. To Fleur, Sir Quentin's aged eccentric mother, Edwina, is sheer delight. She senses that this amazing old lady is not at all unobservant, nor confused. She revels in Edwina's lack of inhibition, and her scorn of the pretentious people around her. Dottie, however, sees Edwina as an appalling nuisance, a bane in the life of Beryl Tims – another English rose – who resentfully looks after her. Dottie also sees Sir Quentin with different eyes from Fleur's: she describes him as reassuring – like a priest she once knew. Fleur is simply amused by this clumsy misreading. But it is clear to the reader that Dottie's stupidity renders her vulnerable to Sir Quentin's power. When Dottie launches into an attack on Fleur's novel, however, Fleur cannot remain dispassionate. Dottie demands that Fleur should clarify the moral identity of her characters; she tells her that 'readers like to know where they stand'. She accuses Fleur of not being womanly and, to show that she is, Fleur succumbs to her fury and throws Dottie out. This display of emotion apart, Fleur is kind to Dottie. Although they see people differently, and although Dottie's husband has been Fleur's lover, Fleur does her best to ensure that there is no animosity between them. In fact, it is through Fleur's efforts to find Dottie some friends that she encourages her to join the Autobiographical Association. It is also to assure Dottie of her good feelings towards her that she reads her part of her novel. Both these steps prove a mistake as far as Fleur is concerned. However, even when Dottie becomes instrumental in the theft of her novel, Fleur has no strong feelings of distaste for her, simply a weary sense of surprise.

Fleur's ability to criticize herself is a strong point in her character. She is perceptive and responsive, but she can also be proud and even bitchy. Her awareness of these shortcomings gives strength to her faith which is, she says, 'abounding'. When she feels particularly impatient and contemptuous towards Beryl Tims, she gives her a present of a brooch Tims admires and of which Fleur is rather fond. But the principal contribution of her faith to her life lies not in good works, but in her sense of wonder. It is beautifully expressed in these lines:

> I remember how the doings of my day appeared again before me, rich and inexplicable life. I fell asleep with a strange sense of sadness and promise meeting and holding hands.

Fleur's delight in life, her deep love for her friend Solly, her affection and admiration for Edwina, and above all her creative response to her experience all contribute to her faith. She distinguishes sharply between her own intuitive recognition of the goodness of life, and Dottie's bureaucratic Catholicism. She sees the latter as an artificial programme, designed to fill the mind with irrelevances and basically to stupefy rather than to stimulate spiritual response:

> I simply don't have time nor the mentality for guilds, indulgences, fasts, feasts and observances. I've never held it right to create more difficulties in matters of religion than already exist.

She detects a polarity between Dottie's concept of faith and her own, and simply decides that if Dottie's were true, hers is false. But the reader is aware that Fleur's spiritual energy raises her above pettiness. Her passion for writing goes together with her love of life; to her as to Cellini, they give her a sense of identity. Fleur says that her novel was taking up 'the sweetest part of her mind'. Writing is like being in love

46

and better. Indeed, her life is so involved with her work that she can't write about one without talking too about the other.

Fleur's creative, generous personality gives this novel its coherence and vivacity. In the end the other characters fade into insignificance and Fleur's *joie de vivre* remains triumphant.

Fleur has few close relationships. The most delightful is with her friend Wally, with whom she dances until four in the morning at Quaglino's. She worked with him in the past, and now he pleases her with amusing anecdotes which lighten her spirits. They have a healthy uncomplicated friendship. Her boyfriend Leslie on the other hand irritates her. She says she is proud of him initially, but, in comparison with the strong personality of Sir Quentin's mother, he appears weak and flaccid to her. She is clearly not in love with him. Unfortunately his wife is obsessed with jealousy for Fleur. She tries to complicate Fleur's life but has little success. Fleur is very charitable to her. Fleur's most important relationship is with her novel, *Warrender Chase*. When she hears of the similarities between what she has written and the events of Sir Quentin's life she is bemused but not unnerved. However, when the typescript disappears she is furious with rage and anxiety. She is not at ease until she has contrived to get it back.

Loitering with Intent asserts the essential independence of the writer. It claims great, almost prophetic insight for the artist. But above all it vindicates the artist's power of moral perception, which enables him or her to see the world in proportion. Fleur's exhilaration as an artist is the driving force behind her involvement with people and her observation as an artist makes it possible to see them in the light of truth. She has no desire to categorize them, but lets them come to her in all their endearing and annoying eccentricity. In this way there is little difference between a positive response to what life has to offer and the ability to create.

Nancy Hawkins: *A Far Cry from Kensington*

A Far Cry from Kensington at first reading appears to recount a series of incidents in a boarding house in Kensington during the early fifties, where the narrator, Nancy Hawkins, was a lodger. However, one of the achievements of the narrative is that the narrator herself is seen to change under the effects of these events. She seems initially to have settled willingly and comfortably into her role of adviser, confidante and gentle friend to all around her. But the forces which come into play in her life in the tall house in South Kensington, and at the offices where she works as a publisher's assistant, effect a change on Nancy, as well as on her friends and colleagues. The skill of the narrative style lies in its conservation of those characteristics which throughout remain part of Nancy Hawkins' identity, and its amused detachment from elements which she had considered permanent but which ultimately she has cause to reject. The change in Nancy together with the enthralling development of personalities and intrigue provide elegant counterpoint in this book.

Nancy presents herself at the beginning of her narrative as an easy-going, dependable woman of twenty-eight. She is 'massive in size', a feature which makes her comfortable and accessible to her acquaintances, who know her as 'Mrs Hawkins'. She appears to have settled into an early middle age, gently gregarious with an affection for the different lodgers in the house, respectful and appreciative of their assorted personalities. She works for a publisher – the Ullswater Press – where she is regarded with a similar affection; although the firm is in financial difficulties and the strain felt by all its employees, Mrs Hawkins is able to dispense calm and reassurance. Without much deliberate involvement on her part she attracts the confidence of Patrick, an intense young book-lover who works for the Ullswater Press, and also the excessive jealousy of his wife. She is bemused by such extreme reaction when, as she says, she has merely 'stood

48

there in my buxom bulk'. Altogether Mrs Hawkins appears to have a well balanced, sensible way of life, disturbed by neither anxieties nor passion.

However, there are features of Nancy Hawkins' character which lie deeper than her relaxed amiability. One of these is her cultivation of insomnia, which she finds delectable. In her 'wide-eyed' midnight she listens lovingly to the silence and finds that she can see her life in perspective, restoring forgotten fragments and dismissing the pressure of immediate circumstances, to focus on matters of greater importance. It is in the night, in these long stretches of unbroken wakefulness that Nancy Hawkins finds her own deep identity. In her narration, she speaks of how she enjoys sleeplessness and that she now looks back at her life in Kensington in these still moments of 'beloved insomnia'. Insomnia is what you make of it, she states decidedly. Clearly her ability to transform what some consider an affliction into a blessing is a sign of a strength of character which is to emerge later in her narrative of events of the early fifties.

Another latent strength of character develops in the course of these events, and indeed precipitates them. Mrs Hawkins, apparently so mild and accommodating, does have a personal passion and this is her respect for and love of good writing.

> It made me sad to leave the galley-proofs of a novel by Cocteau or a new edition of 'Tender is the Night' folded on my desk. Many of the Ullswater Press books were so good, so rare.

While she is at work on her painstaking search for typographical errors, she resents interruptions from Martin York's telephone; he is her boss and he likes to summon her to his office to distract him from his miseries about the imminent collapse of the firm. She can cope with this minor irritation, but one character incurs her savage contempt. He is Hector Bartlett, whom she has known since her first days in the publishing world. Hector Bartlett is a social poseur but, more nauseating still, he has literary pretensions. His obsession with publishing leads him to write copiously on anything that occurs to him, without sensitivity or purpose. It was his habit to waylay Nancy Hawkins in an effort to secure her influence. Although occasionally she is amused by his clumsy poses, on one occasion she is startled and annoyed at being disturbed from her reverie, walking in Green Park. He suddenly confronts her, and continues to aggravate her with his tortuous account of how he intends to turn a novel into a film script. Ultimately her composure disintegrates. '*Pisseur de copie*!' she hisses at him. This insult, which summarizes her hatred of his facile approach to writing, decides their relationship throughout the book. Hector Bartlett is mortified by these words, and promptly puts into action every device he can think of to destroy Mrs Hawkins. One word to his friend, a famous novelist, means that Nancy loses her job.

The conflict between Nancy Hawkins and the '*pisseur de copie*' is based on more than personal antagonism. Bartlett arouses her contempt through his opportunism, and through his literary pretensions: he knows titles and names of authors, but essentially he has read little. More fundamentally, she feels a moral disgust for him. She sees clearly how he is capable of undermining other people, of influencing them, merely because they don't have the courage or the strength to oppose him:

> ... a great many people fell in with Hector's pretensions, a surprising number, especially those simple souls who quell their doubts because they cannot bring themselves to discern a blatant pose; the effort would be too wearing and wearying, and might call for an open challenge and lead to unpleasantness.

However, Nancy Hawkins takes up this challenge with her uncharacteristic insult. In treating this man with such scorn, she does indeed lay herself open to unpleasantness, but her inner strength of character enables her to survive. She is conscious of her tendency to make moral judgments, and believes that she is the stronger for this ability:

It is my happy element to judge between right and wrong
regardless of what I might actually do. At the same time, the
wreaking of vengeance and the imposing of justice on others
and on myself are not at all in my line. It is enough for me
to discriminate mentally and leave the rest to God.

When she speaks of her 'happy element', she implies that her
observations of the moral character of people's behaviour give
her pleasure; however, she is by no means convinced that she is
necessarily right. Her statement that she is reluctant to involve
herself directly in the outcome of events shows a capacity
for self-questioning, and a very fundamental faith. She will
eventually have cause to question several of her judgments.

Nancy Hawkins' involvement with Hector Bartlett extends
far beyond the area of which she is aware. She is ready to
lose her job for exercising her free will when she insults him.
Throughout the book she refuses to retract the insult, although
pressed, and indeed derives pleasure from repeating it. She
loses two jobs as a result, jobs which are dear to her, and
without which she is depressed, spending her time riding round
suburban London on buses. However, she does not see any
reason to link the despicable Hector Bartlett with her fellow
lodger, Wanda Podolak, whose tribulations provide the only
diversion from the problems at the office. Wanda has received
an anonymous letter from a mysterious person calling themself
'An Organiser'. In this letter, she is accused of not declaring her
income to the authorities. The simple Polish dressmaker, whom
Nancy Hawkins had admired for her generosity and sociability
with frequently calling compatriots, is confused and distressed
by this letter. Nancy Hawkins and Milly, her landlady, do their
best to work out who could have sent it, but one by one they
eliminate their fellow lodgers. When, eventually, Wanda receives
an anonymous phone-call, Nancy and Milly are relieved; the
call came from outside the house one evening when all the
lodgers were in. It was 'not one of us, not one of us', Nancy
Hawkins repeats to herself. She is buoyed up by this sense

of solidarity, forgetting momentarily Wanda's misery, and less intent on finding its cause. That evening, as she dances in the moonlight with William, a fellow lodger, on Milly's lawn, Nancy Hawkins enjoys the 'great lightness' that has fallen on the house. Wanda's plight seems remote. She writes, in retrospect:

> Hector Bartlett was already far from my thoughts; there was no possible way I could have thought of him in connection with Wanda ... But even if I had known, it would have been irrelevant to my feeling of relief ...

For all her well-balanced integrity, Nancy Hawkins had at that time a limited perspective. Her concern for Wanda was bound up with a need of security in the lodging house, and of confidence in her fellow lodgers. The *bonhomie* that prevailed in Milly's house had obviously made it a home to Nancy, these years of early widowhood. She admits that all the lodgers subsequently lost interest in identifying Wanda's persecutor, although they had not forgotten the mystery. But they were 'all too busy with the foreground of our lives to notice what was happening to Wanda'.

However, the 'snail trail' of Hector Bartlett's sinister activities is winding its course, although it is to be a long time before Nancy will connect him with Wanda's distress. Her distaste for Bartlett is, as far as she is aware, roused most strongly by his pretentiousness. But, at the firm of Mackintosh and Tooley, where she finds her next job, she encounters another source of unpleasantness, which will eventually relate to Hector Bartlett. Ian Tooley, one of Nancy's new employers, possesses a small black box which he keeps in his office and which he explains operates 'radionically'. It has a row of coloured lights and a few knobs. There is also a place to insert a piece of hair or a blood smear from the person it was intended to affect. Ian Tooley had trained his assistant Abigail to operate it. He assures Nancy Hawkins that treatment by the Box could cure all ailments. Both Abigail and Nancy are highly sceptical about his claims, and Nancy regards the Box as devoid of any functional possibility. She points out, however, in order to qualify Ian Tooley's insistence on its powerful properties, that if it could do good, it could also do evil. She is curious to know what Abigail has been asked to do with the Box, and whom she is trying to affect. But Abigail tells her that the matter is highly confidential: to her, the role of operating the Box is merely part of her job.

Nancy Hawkins' job with Mackintosh and Tooley is illuminating to her in a far more powerful way than anything the Box could instigate. She notices that all the employees have some grotesque feature; one has a stammer, another a livid strawberry mark on her face, and so on. Thinking about this one night, Nancy starts to wonder what it was about her that had qualified her for employment at the firm; it is clear to her that the staff had been chosen not in spite of their oddities, but because of them. She gets out of bed, turns on the light, and looks at herself in the mirror. It strikes her that she is, in fact, massively overweight. This was the reason why she had been chosen by Mackintosh and Tooley. No one would voice a complaint against such a person; she is one of their 'alibis'. This realization has a sudden and decisive effect on Nancy: she will diet. From then on she will eat only half of everything she normally eats. Her decision, about which she tells no one, is as profound as her condemnation of Hector Bartlett; the overtly easy going, comfortable Mrs Hawkins has a will of iron.

Nancy becomes more attractive; men are interested in her; she is constantly told how well she looks. Her problems are not over, since Hector Bartlett reappears. Through his novelist friend, Emma Loy, he has presented a book to Nancy's employers, and Nancy has been asked to edit it. She finds *The Eternal Quest* as nauseating as its author and agrees with her fellow lodger, the medical student, William, that it is 'a lot of balls': mere waffle of names and second-hand opinion, with no knowledge or understanding of the writers discussed. Her refusal to edit it costs her this job. She acquiesces, but decides that she is beginning to weary of the publishing world. Meanwhile another quandary has developed: Isobel, one of the lodgers in Milly's house, announces that she is pregnant. She apparently has no clear knowledge of who the father can be. Her father calls a meeting of Isobel's fellow lodgers, which turns into a party. Isobel is not at all distressed by her pregnancy; they all agree that she should not have an abortion, everyone offers to help and they all enjoy sherry and snacks together. As Nancy leaves, she is bewildered to encounter Wanda on the landing, apparently in great distress. She brings Nancy into her room where lies open a box, like the one Alec Tooley had shown Nancy. Nancy had already noticed this box in Wanda's room when her clothes were being adjusted after her loss of weight, but only had a slight suspicion that the box was the same as the one she had seen. Now it was clear: Wanda worked the Box. Wanda's state of mind this evening is quite wild. Hysterically she accuses Nancy of plotting against her with the other tenants. She speaks directly of her Box, claiming she makes no money from it but merely uses it to heal the sick. More alarmingly, she wails that Nancy is wasting and will die. To calm her down, Nancy tells her that she will ring Fr Stanislas, but the mention of the priest's name has a devastating effect on Wanda, who now starts to scream. Nancy decides she cannot cope. William comes out to help, but Wanda has locked herself in her room. Later Nancy confides in William that Wanda's strange predictions have made her feel 'spooky'. William informs her that she needs a sex life and proceeds to remedy this deficiency. Her affair with William starts at this point, and all anxiety about Wanda and the Box is swept aside.

Nancy's last encounter with Wanda is when Wanda comes out of her room, trying to find out who Nancy is talking to on the phone. It is in fact Emma Loy, but Wanda is convinced it must be Fr Stanislas. Again she accuses Nancy of plotting against her. Nancy is alarmed by Wanda's behaviour; she is conscious of backing away from her, of fearing 'psychic contagion'. She and William agree that something must be done to help Wanda and Nancy goes to the Oratory to find Fr Stanislas' number, which she writes on a piece of paper and puts in her bag. Then she goes to meet the exciting, successful, but morally fallible Emma Loy. After a challenging and revealing talk, Nancy walks back through Green Park. She returns to the house to find that Wanda has drowned herself.

Wanda's death is a shock, and brings home to Nancy her ignorance and her impotence. She has seen Wanda's behaviour merely from her own viewpoint; the anonymous letter caused Wanda acute anxiety, which Nancy understood, but she had decided Wanda's continued distress was an exaggeration: 'Oh God! She might milk this affair for the rest of her life,' she had thought. Subsequently, Nancy had found the change in Wanda curious, but attributable to some kind of breakdown. She was ageing and fading, Nancy had decided. But on another later occasion, Nancy had also noticed that there might be something sexually attractive about Wanda. She saw her in bed with her corn-coloured hair down. The news of Wanda's death causes Nancy great self-reproach. She had sensed that Wanda needed to talk to a priest and tells herself that, had she contacted Fr Stanislas in time, Wanda might have been saved. When going over the contents of Wanda's room with Greta, her sister, she discovers what she takes to be a suit of Hector Bartlett's. Suddenly, she has an insight into Wanda's great misfortune. Hector Bartlett has seduced her and has been using her. William later rejects this theory, and tells her that the suit is in fact his. But she is now convinced that there is a fundamental link between the '*pisseur de copie*', the Box and Wanda's death. It later emerges that Bartlett has often visited Wanda, telling Milly that he is a cousin of hers, training to be a priest. Nancy finds grotesque photographs of them, their bodies in faked poses. Further search reveals fake press cuttings, recounting a story of police investigation into a Polish dressmaker treating with radionics a young woman living in the same house who was dangerously losing weight and wasting away. Nancy sees clearly that Bartlett is behind this fabrication, and that he was the source of the unbearable pressure on Wanda.

Nancy had sensed the moral depravity in the '*pisseur de copie*', she had disliked the idea of the Box, she had been aware of Wanda's emotional instability, but she had never connected these factors. Now that she is involved with William, she realizes that her perception has been sharpened. She understands Wanda's vulnerability in a way that had never crossed her mind before. Wanda had no protection against an ageing woman's suscep- tibility and, by exploiting this aspect of Wanda's personality, Bartlett had persuaded her to 'work the Box' against Nancy. Through this 'black magic' he had virtually enslaved Wanda, cutting her off from her chatty sociability with her fellow Poles, from her successful dressmaking work, and from her religion. In a sense Bartlett's conquest of Wanda is a defeat too for Nancy. Her confidence in her own understanding had made her into a moralizer, questioning herself little. Her realization of how her obesity had made her a freak, employable for that reason by Mackintosh and Tooley, leads her to change her life. She dieted to reject the image of herself that she had suddenly been compelled to confront. The revelation of Bartlett's seduction of Wanda has a similar effect. Nancy realizes how little she had understood of Wanda's situation, of her sexuality. 'What did I really know of all the people I had met in the offices where I had worked, day after day?' Nancy had cast Wanda into an image as restrictive as that from which she has liberated herself:

> . . . I saw, and didn't see. I had thought of Wanda as the plump, Polish dress-maker, her life full of church and friends and enemies, of Madonnas and novenas and her ladies who came for fittings. The last thing I would have thought was that she might have a lover.

Nevertheless, the facts of Wanda's plight now reveal themselves to Nancy through her intuition. What is discovered in Wanda's room, the photographs, the fake press cuttings, merely confirm Nancy's suspicions. However, it had taken Wanda's death to instigate Nancy's reassessment of her original assumptions.

The story of *A Far Cry from Kensington* has several riveting features: anonymous letters and phone calls, the mysterious Box and its occult implications, an unexpected love affair. But the coherence of the book is substantially moral. Nancy Hawkins was an unadventurous, undemanding and in some ways complacent person. Although only twenty-eight, she was happy to pass as older, accepting seats offered her on the bus when it was full. When, in the course of the book, she recounts the few weeks of her wartime marriage, it is clear that it was a devastating experience which in a sense immured her from any further movement towards emotional involvement. Not only was her husband killed in action, but their last night together was traumatic: Tom had got drunk and was violent, breaking furniture and hurting Nancy. Now, ten years later, she did not think of relationships with men, having subconsciously rejected the possibility. When Hugh Lederer, Isobel's father, invites her out to lunch, she is momentarily light-hearted at the idea, only to find that he, too, wants only her advice and help with placing Isobel in publishing; he is not interested in her as a woman. Nancy accepts this. It is not until her reflections on the conditions of employment by Mackintosh and Tooley that she decides to change. Subsequently she decides that she has had enough not only of being too fat, but of giving advice. She starts to say that she can't cope. She refuses, privately, to offer any more assistance to Isobel. And when she and William are looking for a flat, she happily and selfishly decides on the basement flat of her new employers in Highgate, which is more convenient for her than for William. From her brief but memorable discovery of her husband's violence she has given herself a piece of advice: people should see the worst side of one another first. Fortunately William is happy to go along with her arrangement; what he teases her about is her doling out of advice, her readiness to take on other people's problems. At these times he calls her 'Mrs Hawkins' and she is easily persuaded to snap out of her role of moral mentor to all. Both her own strength of will and her relationship with William have led Nancy to break out of the fat, comfortable identity she had created for herself.

57

Two aspects of Nancy's personality are not changed but strengthened by the experiences she has in Kensington in the fifties. One is her love of books, the sole element in her life that was fundamental at that time. Not only does this lead to her notorious insult of Hector Bartlett, it also brings her to a deep wisdom about the world of writing and publishing. She muses on the number of writers 'who still have in their drawers the leaf-eared typescripts that they sent to sea in a sieve'. She tells an aspiring author that he must not generalize, but write about something in particular. When asked whether Proust did this, she responds that he wrote 'about everything in particular'. It is clear that her perception in matters of writing leads her to develop the approach which is now implicit in her actual narrative. Personal integrity provides the meaning of experience; isolated incidents mean nothing until they are evaluated and responded to; hence the value of the 'wide-eyed midnight' musing.

A fundamental element in Nancy's life is her faith, and this too develops in the course of her experiences in Kensington. Initially she had a mere habitual faith; it led to her reciting automatically the Angelus every midday. Ultimately she decides that this is as superstitious as the Box. But some aspects of her faith are not superstitious; they are at the heart of her understanding. When Emma Loy tells her that she believes some days and not others, Nancy decides that if she were in such a case she would 'have a jolly good time the days I believed and repent the days I didn't'. Faith to Nancy is a cause for rejoicing; she says to William that 'she couldn't not believe', and he tells her cheerfully that she would have to believe for both of them.

Nancy Hawkins is the first woman character Muriel Spark has created who reaches a point in her maturity that enables her consciously to change her life. Her perception of others extends to become a perception of herself. Whereas she is initially contented to have a comfortable image in the eyes of others, she realizes that she is cheating. By watering down her responses, she is denying her real identity. She makes a decision to change. She slims, she becomes involved in a

58

relationship with William and most importantly she rids herself of her complacency. Wanda's tragic plight makes her realize the inadequacy of her understanding.

Conclusion

An important indication of Muriel Spark's skill as a writer is her ability to create characters who, while running into similar problems and challenges, conserve their own identity. All the women I have discussed above are substantially different, not merely as a result of their circumstances, but as a result of their individuality.

Caroline Rose is the most neurotic; she is frightened of her mind. Her experience is disturbing, but the maturity she develops as a consequence of it means that she emerges triumphant. She is willing to accept the complex fusion of the life around her and her artistic ability to observe it and define it.

January Marlow, like Caroline, looks for companionship in a man. But, unlike Caroline, she finds a relationship that has a stimulating spiritual value. She is consequently able to grow; she reflects on her outlook and, on many occasions, adjusts her attitudes. She admits to elements of superstition in her own habits of faith, she admits to stupid squeamishness in refusing to take things she needs which have been left by passengers killed on the plane. Most importantly, she recognizes her own emotional susceptibility, her unwarranted readiness to get annoyed, for example. Her development is, however, a tribute to her self-sufficiency. She does not become dependent on Robinson; she learns from him.

Barbara Vaughan is certainly the most passionate of Spark's maturing women characters. Her passion is related to her faith. It enables her to leap into the unknown and to expose herself to experiences which, in earlier days, she would have shunned.

At several points in the narrative, it is suggested that she has considerable intellectual gifts. But Muriel Spark is careful not to portray her as constantly evaluating her situation. The third person narrative is useful in this. Spark is able to tell us: '. . . her habits of mind could not cope with her experience.' Unlike Caroline Rose and January Marlow, Barbara has come to live in terms of a deeply passionate sensibility. The impression given is that this sensibility finds its expression above all in her faith, the outcome of both her English and Jewish formation. Her relationships take second place to this and the importance of her career is negligible. Barbara has a stronger personality than Caroline and January; the impact she makes is not merely through the cleverness of her remarks but through her intensity. This is reflected through the response to her of the English consul, Freddy, who finds her cold and terrifying. He also observes that for some reason she makes him think of religion. The statement that Muriel Spark is an unemotive, calculating writer is given the lie by her creation of Barbara who, to attain credibility in the minds of Spark's readers, demands respect for her intensely passionate nature.

Fleur Talbot is the one joyful and resilient woman amongst those in whose minds we are invited to share. On this occasion the first person narrative conveys, not the isolation of January Marlow, but the conviviality of the narrator. Fleur's exuberance is very much part of her personality but it is also a highly significant trait. Above all it is linked with her love of writing. Her author's mind, which delights in experience, gives her a soaring independence; everything that happens to her enriches her creativity. Unlike Caroline Rose, who is fearful of her mind's apparent autonomy in composing and narrating experience, Fleur relishes it. The fusion between life and her writing, more explicitly described than in *The Comforters*, is something Fleur wonders at and then takes for granted. Fleur is not a character who changes radically in the course of the narrative; her salient qualities are adaptable and she is sustained by her constant readiness to respond and to enjoy. It is not only her exuberance that endears her to the reader. Her powers of perception are very skilfully portrayed; where other characters in the novel are blind or deluded, Fleur sees clearly. The suggestion is that an artist's insight is a gift of grace.

Nancy Hawkins is not a writer, but her affable, easy-going personality is presented strongly through a narrative idiom of intimate communication. Just as Mrs Hawkins is everybody's friend, so is she the reader's. Because of her unmannered, relaxed account, she is accessible to the reader who shares her perception of others. Mrs Hawkins has two important gifts: she is able to form moral judgments but, more importantly, she is able to be self-critical. We watch while she recounts how she readjusts the focus of her life and humbly admits where she has been mistaken. In Mrs Hawkins' case her relationship with a man is extremely important in her development. William's involvement with her confirms that she has been able to emerge from the restrictions of her previous self-imposed image. He restores her youth although, in a sense, she herself has been most instrumental in doing this. While she presents herself as an easy-going person, it is in fact her passionate response to Hector Bartlett that triggers off the events of the narrative.

These women then are all very different. But the novels in which they play the central part show us the landscape where Muriel Spark identifies her points of reference. They show us, too, elements of a profound wisdom which, although it is not summarized nor in any way presented as dogma, emerges as a *modus vivendi*. All these women reject an intellectual, categoric way of explaining life. They all admit to the essential shortness of their view and they all have a need of faith to establish proportions which exceed their human limitations. Although they have male friends, lovers even, who bring them companionship and who lighten their minds, essentially they depend on themselves.

— 2 —

WOMEN OF POWER

These women are witty and sardonic creations. They convey much of Muriel Spark's wisdom and her capacity to observe and analyse relationships. It is possible that the novels in which they feature have been the least accessible to Spark's casual readers. In two cases, *The Prime of Miss Jean Brodie* and *The Abbess of Crewe*, the main protagonists have such powerful personalities that they can blur the perspective of the narrative. However, when reviewed carefully, a moral profile emerges which identifies them in terms beyond the immediate impact they make. Spark focuses beyond scandal and glamour. In the novels I have considered in the previous section which recount the experience of sensitive minds, the question of power and of its exploitation for evil ends arises often. January Marlow in *Robinson* has an instinctive dislike of Tom Wells; she discovers later that he is prepared to fabricate a false account of Robinson's disappearance, and also that he is prepared to kill her. Subsequently, on her return to England, she learns that he has been running a lucrative business exploiting people's superstitious credulity. There is no doubt about the animosity this character arouses. Similarly, Fleur Talbot in *Loitering with Intent* intuitively detects something evil in the intentions of her employer, Sir Quentin. It emerges that he is manipulating those weak enough to be drawn into his power, and that he exploits their vulnerability and their credulity. Fleur is contemptuous of him, yet furious too when she finds he has arranged for her novel to be stolen. Fleur remarks in her narrative that artists, at some time or other, invariably come

62

into contact with 'pure evil'. *Loitering with Intent* is a vindication of the artist's moral perception.

Nancy Hawkins in *A Far Cry from Kensington* takes issue with Hector Bartlett for his philistine approach to writing in which there is no sensitivity nor authenticity. Her loathing of the '*pisseur de copie*' is justified further when his horrific exploitation of Wanda comes to light.

However, there is no catalyst in the books about women of power. The reader is the observer; his or her responses must decide the ultimate impact of the character. Muriel Spark's characterization is so brilliant that within the character herself are found the contractions and negative impulses which signal to the reader abuse of power. To be aware of these it is essential to be sensitive to the character's motivation and the dynamics of her behaviour. Laughter is a response that provides a good guide.

Jean Brodie: *The Prime of Miss Jean Brodie*

Miss Brodie in *The Prime of Miss Jean Brodie* is a character of devastating impact. Her statements are epigrammatic, her confidence apparently boundless and her influence so compulsive that the girls that she chooses as her favourites become 'hers for life' as she says. In many ways Miss Brodie is attractive to the reader who is affected by the response of other characters largely besotted by her. Her ability to explode conventional attitudes ('Safety does not come first. Goodness, truth and beauty come first.') is a sign of her independence. Her passion for certain figures like Giotto and Pavlova is essential in her life and her desire to impart it to her girls appears generous and admirable. Her method of teaching is highly personal and involves an account of her own experiences including her love life; it is as if she wished to relive these experiences with her pupils and share with them the lessons she has learned. Not surprisingly, the girls she has chosen identify themselves in the terms she imposes. They see her as 'the dangerous Miss Brodie', both alarmed and excited by the way in which she sweeps conventional education aside and provides what she considers to be more stimulating and worthwhile material. Just as the girls she teaches are overwhelmed by her, so the two masters at the school, the art and the music master, are smitten by her, and their infatuation is no less extreme. As the book develops, the consequences of these relationships emerge, as do the implications of Jean Brodie's attitudes. The woman who first appears as an indomitable personality, prepared to resist all questioners of her unorthodox methods, is slowly defeated – not by her enemies, but by her mistaken assumption that her power is absolute.

The initial impression of Miss Brodie's power is conveyed largely by the effect she has on her pupils. Unquestioning and uncritical, they absorb all she says, and the hostility of intruders into the classroom gives her words extra magic. The little clique of Miss Brodie and her girls constitutes its own self-protection. It is clear from the beginning that there is no element of dialogue in Miss Brodie's teaching; in fact, it is quite authoritarian:

'Who is the greatest Italian painter?'
'Leonardo da Vinci, Miss Brodie.'
'That is incorrect. The answer is Giotto, he is my favourite.'

The only criterion of success offered the girls is Miss Brodie's favour and their response is merely a repetition of her dogmatic pronouncements. She grandly defines her concept of education as 'a leading out of what is already there in the pupil's soul'. However, the reader can see that Miss Brodie dominates her pupils rather than endeavouring in any way to respond to innate gifts. She claims that she has no intention of putting ideas into their heads, but we read from their well-documented fantasies that their minds are filled with her terms and with her preoccupations. There is a paradox in her conviction that she is enriching the lives of her girls while being at the same time resentful of any interest they might have in anything or anyone beyond what she herself knows and values. When they pass into the upper school she is concerned lest any of her girls should become attached to one of the senior mistresses: it is clear that her attitude to them is keenly possessive and that she depends on their devotion for her own self-assurance. Her desire to keep an absolute control over her girls makes her vitriolic if any of them departs from her sphere of influence and pursues activities or ideas for which she has no sympathy. Eunice, for example, is treated with scorn for opting for the modern side of the upper school course and for involving herself in the Episcopalian Church, preparing for confirmation. Miss Brodie tells her scathingly that she will end up as a Girl Guide leader and live in a suburb like Costorphine, where Eunice in fact does live.

Miss Brodie openly rejects what is taught in other classes, and disregards the syllabus she herself is supposed to follow, merely pretending to teach in an orthodox way when visited by the headmistress. When exams come around, she simply tells the girls to 'try to scrape through, even if you learn up the stuff and forget it the next day.' She dismisses out of hand all knowledge which is not part of her own way of thinking: 'Art and religion first; then philosophy; lastly science.'

It is revealed to us early in the novel that the selection of Miss Brodie's favourites is not based on her perception of their individual gifts, nor even their personal appeal, but on 'shabby principles'. It was merely a question of expediency:

Miss Brodie had already selected her favourites, or rather those whom she could trust; or rather those whose parents she could trust not to lodge complaints about the more advanced and seditious aspects of her educational policy . . .

Miss Brodie's idea of teaching is essentially dogmatic; her perspective is hers alone and she expects humble acceptance rather than understanding. Her girls learn more about her than anything else, and what they learn is based on her own self-portrait in which she appears to reign over all. The girls amplify what she says to them in amusing but grotesque fantasies about themselves and essentially about her. Their imagination rather than their intellect is fired. She manages to mystify rather than to inform.

The weaknesses in Miss Brodie's approach to education are the result of her moral make-up rather than any conscious ideological intention. She is so self-absorbed that it never occurs to her to depart from this obsession; indeed, she considers it totally justifiable to impart her every prejudice to her pupils simply because they are hers. In her rare narratorial interventions, Muriel Spark makes it clear that Miss Brodie is one of a certain type of woman to be found in the 1930s, a type who is rarely concerned with teaching:

> There were legions of her kind during the nineteen thirties, women from the age of thirty and upwards, who crowded their war-bereaved spinsterhood with voyages of discovery into new ideas and energetic practices in art or social welfare, education or religion.

Spark recounts that such women lived according to their own lights, offering advice on painting and birth control to their neighbours, attending lectures and pursuing ardently their philanthropic and enlightened interests, totally confident of the enlightenment of their approach: 'And so, seen in this light, there was nothing outwardly odd about Miss Brodie.' It is the contrast between her and the rest of the staff at Marcia Blaine's that causes her to stand out so vividly in her environment. The basic difference between her and her colleagues is defined as her 'state of fluctuating development', whereas they had stopped questioning.

It is interesting that Muriel Spark speaks of this arrogant, assertive person as in a state of fluctuating development. The dogmatic tone of Miss Brodie's remarks suggests that she is fully decided and has no need to reflect further on the basic truths of life. Her confidence appears above all to be in herself; she constantly reminds her pupils that she is 'in her prime', fully developed in her tastes and in her judgments. Muriel Spark tells us, surprisingly in view of Miss Brodie's apparent unorthodoxy, that she is 'an Edinburgh spinster of the deepest dye', adhering strictly to Church of Scotland habits. She attends classes on comparative religion and recommends reading the Gospels to her girls. However, her religious sensibility (if such it may be called) gives her no clear moral perspective. She has no humility and is certain only that 'God was on her side'. In fact, her sense of religion serves to add a metaphysical aura to her own observations; she is her own God. For this reason she has no compunction in sleeping with the music master, and in hoping that one of her pupils will sleep with the art master, with whom Miss Brodie is in love. We are told that Miss Brodie's girls see her actions as 'outside the context of right and wrong' and Rose – the pupil Miss Brodie intends to see become the art master's lover – is encouraged by her to assume a similar exemption from conventional moral standards.

Miss Brodie sees herself as the source of truth and never doubts this. However, her plans misfire, her girls grow beyond her reach, her lover marries another teacher, her favourite pupil becomes a Roman Catholic and – something she has not imagined possible – she is 'betrayed'. The headmistress acquires evidence that she is a fascist and has persuaded one of the girls to go to fight for Franco, as a result of which the girl is killed in a train accident. The grimmest feature of this betrayal is that clearly one of her schoolgirl confidantes has supplied the damning information. She spends the rest of her life wondering who this could have been.

The traitor is Sandy, the most perceptive of Miss Brodie's girls, who slowly develops a capacity to appraise her teacher critically. Indeed, one of her first observations is generated by an outing through the slums of Edinburgh, when she suddenly perceives the group as 'Miss Brodie's fascisti . . . not to the naked eye, marching along, but all knit together for her need and in another way, marching along.' It occurs to her that Miss Brodie's antagonism towards the Girl Guides is based on jealousy towards a rival group of fascisti. Then she hastily dismisses the thought 'because she loved Miss Brodie'. It is as a fascist that Miss Brodie loses her job, although her way of thinking is presented in the book more in quasi-religious than in political terms. It is true that she frequently dwells on her admiration for Mussolini, and commends Hitler very highly, calling him a 'prophet-figure like Thomas Carlyle', but the essence of her attitude, as Sandy perceives but does not attempt to explain to the headmistress, is related to Calvinism. Calvin denied the individual free will and saw all events as predestined. Miss Brodie, like Calvin's God, holds sway over her pupils and expects each step of their lives to fulfil her expectations. Sandy, as she grows older, senses this attitude in her teacher. She realizes that Miss Brodie has 'elected herself to grace', pursuing a path of no less 'exotic suicidal enchantment' than if she had taken to drink. Sandy learns that Calvin saw the human soul as blindly enslaved to sin, and granted some people an 'erroneous sense of joy and salvation', only to have a nasty surprise when their lives came to an end.

It is Miss Brodie's conviction of her incontestable righteousness, her lack of humility that irritates Sandy. A narratorial observation emphasizes this: 'Just as an excessive sense of guilt can drive people to excessive action, so was Miss Brodie driven to it by an excessive lack of guilt.' Sandy is fascinated by Miss Brodie's obsession with the need for Rose, another favourite pupil, to sleep with the art master. Sandy is aware how little Miss Brodie really knows Rose, who is quite happy to model for the art master, but has no idea of taking matters further. Sandy sees the folly of her teacher in making all these plans and in seeing Rose as an extension of herself. Movingly, Sandy finds a beauty in Miss Brodie in this time of folly:

Sandy felt warmly towards Miss Brodie at those times when she saw how she was misled in her idea of Rose. It was then that Miss Brodie looked beautiful and fragile . . .

However, a little later, when Sandy faults Miss Brodie's plans, by sleeping herself with the art master, she begins to see the situation from a different perspective. She ultimately forgets the man, but takes his religion, and starts to think as a Catholic. At this time Miss Brodie's intention of controlling her pupils' lives appears even more odious to her: 'She thinks she is Providence, thought Sandy, she thinks she is the God of Calvin, she sees the beginning and the end.'

When Miss Brodie tells Sandy that it was she who persuaded the impressionable Joyce Emily to go to Spain to join the Civil War, this horrific action fires Sandy into betraying her teacher. 'Fuming with Christian morals', she tells her headmistress that Miss Brodie is a 'born Fascist'. Accused of teaching fascism, Miss Brodie is compelled to retire at the end of the summer term.

One of the skills of Muriel Spark's narrative is that the reader is invited to have a compassion for Miss Brodie, as well as a sense of outrage at her self-assertive, domineering manner. Sandy, eventually recovered from her phase of moral righteousness, looks back at Miss Brodie and recognizes how much she has underestimated her teacher:

> It was twenty-five years before Sandy had so far recovered from a creeping vision of disorder that she could look back and recognize that Miss Brodie's defective sense of self-criticism had not been without its beneficent and enlarging effects . . .

Miss Brodie's mistake in assuming she could control and predestine her pupils' lives is made very plain to the reader, yet it is also clear that she herself is the most damaged victim of her folly. The picture of her at the end of her life is distressing:

'Miss Brodie sat shrivelled and betrayed in her long preserved dark musquash coat . . .', and her blind groping for the truth of who betrayed her emphasizes her sense of impotence and defeat. The pathos of her downfall enforces the theme of her basic inadequacy, which she herself would never contemplate, but which threads through the book. It is here that the Catholic perspective of moral disarray is a major factor in the presentation of Miss Brodie. Only by seeing the temptation to place absolute confidence in limited human judgment as a sin from which we suffer, can Miss Brodie be forgiven and pitied. At one point Muriel Spark intervenes openly in the narrative to state that only in the Roman Catholic Church could Miss Brodie's extreme temperament have found a context which both admitted it and pacified it:

> . . . she was by temperament suited only to the Roman Catholic church; possibly it could have embraced, even while it disciplined, her soaring and diving spirit, it might even have normalized her.

But Miss Brodie was never released from her illusion that her own judgment could provide her with an absolute truth. The narrowness of her view is brought home by Muriel Spark's description of the experience of two of her pupils, freed from the teacher's influence, and overcome by the boundless possibilities of life. When Sandy became a Catholic like the art master: 'Her mind was full of his religion as a night sky is full of things visible and invisible . . .' and Jenny, much later in her life, was suddenly attracted by a man she sees in Rome: 'the concise happening filled her with astonishment whenever it came to mind in later days, and with a sense of the hidden possibilities in all things.' Miss Brodie has no sense of the infinite freedom of existence and this is the cause of her lack of humility. Her one moment of regret comes very late in her life, when it occurs to her that she treated Mary Macgregor, one of her set, unkindly. Indeed, Mary was constantly upbraided and chided throughout her school life, 'a nobody whom everybody could blame'. Once, on an outing with Miss Brodie, Sandy was tempted to be pleasant to Mary, but then repressed this, 'since by this action she would separate herself and be lonely and blameable'. Miss Brodie's ultimate reflection that she had been unkind to Mary is a conscious change of mind, although her judgments have been unstable and inconsistent throughout her years with the girls. At one point Muriel Spark comments: 'the principles governing her at the end of her prime would have astonished her at the beginning of it'. She denies the changeability of her mind, and yet it is her most human feature – and, as Muriel Spark points out, her fluctuating development distinguished her from her blinkered colleagues. Nevertheless, she fails to appreciate her own inconsistencies.

The character of Miss Brodie is presented with wit, wisdom and compassion. Her passions are intense and dangerous, but her desire to share them is generous rather than sinister. She clearly believed that she had dedicated her prime to her girls, and quite genuinely gave them all she could. As Sandy remarks from her convent, 'She was quite innocent in her way.'

Miss Brodie's power is no more sinister than that of any educationalist; indeed, it is less so, since she does not exert power from behind a syllabus or through threat of examination failure, but through her own passion for what she values in life. In this sense, she can be seen as altruistic. But she fails utterly to see that she is indulging herself at the expense of the freedom of others. She commits the error of playing God, of assuming that everyone she chooses will fall under her control. Because of her vast assumptions and her unquestioning prejudice, Miss Brodie is in many ways a comic character. But she is also a threatening character, since no character in the book fails to submit to the effects of her strong personality, except those who are far blinder and far more limited than she. Ultimately however, she is pathetic. Not only has she lost her power, but she has no ability to understand why the lives of those she nurtured have developed so very differently from the way she had planned.

Alexandra: *The Abbess of Crewe*

The Abbess of Crewe is a satire, clearly linked with the Watergate case of 1973, yet its theme is basically moral and cannot be interpreted merely by reference to specific events or personalities. The Watergate scandal is brought to mind by several features of the story: bugging, fabrication of scenario, deletion of particular expressions (in this case, poetry) from recordings. However, the fundamental similarity between the Watergate case and the scandal at Crewe lies in the implication of a system of power without integrity, far more sinister than the machinations of any individual. The fact that Richard Nixon, President of the USA, and Alexandra, Abbess of Crewe, were able to change at will the presentation of the truth, calls into question the system within which these powerful figures operate. The fact that each was successful for so long suggests an unquestioning compliance from those beneath them. Just as the Watergate case showed how little respect there was in government circles for the privacy and security of individuals, so *The Abbess of Crewe* presents a world in which the notions of truth and integrity are so obscured that the Abbess can gain a total power, and in fact define herself all the terms within which she expects those beneath her to operate. The exposure of the Watergate break-in and Nixon's eventual confession of the falsehoods he had perpetrated were sufficient to bring about the downfall of the Republican party, at least for the time being. But *The Abbess of Crewe* does not have a political target. Nor is its target a single personality, although Alexandra's arrogance, her contempt for the other nuns, her self-centred amorality are all shown to flourish unchallenged in the context of the convent. What emerges from the book is an indictment of those elements within the Roman Catholic Church which remained unresponsive to the second Vatican Council and encouraged servile piety and acquiescence instead of valuing personal experience of each member of the Church in the way that Pope John had recommended.

72

The character of Alexandra domineers throughout the book. Her most impressive feature is her remoteness. Her close companions do not converse with her; they merely echo what she says. Her beauty and dignity are emphasized, the narrator often pausing to dwell on these. She is a 'tower of ivory', a 'Lombardy poplar', sweeping majestically through the convent, aloof and opaque. We are told nothing about her inner mind; the narrator joins the reader in marvelling at the obscurity of her thoughts: 'She looks at the file of tombs . . . thinking of who knows what occupant, past or to come . . .'. All we are told about her interior life is that she sings English poetry in place of the verses of the Holy Office. This suggests a passionate, personal dimension in her character, but beyond the recitation of the poetry, such a dimension is never developed. It also asserts her indifference to the terms of the religious rites. She calls poetry her 'passion', commending her sisters each to her 'own source of grace'. It is clear that poetry provides for Alexandra the only appropriate vehicle for the states of mind which she experiences. 'I am in love with English poetry; even my devotions take that form.'

We learn about the personality and influence of Alexandra from the way she lives in the convent and from her relationship with the other nuns. Her 'closest nuns', Mildred and Walburga, are finely tuned to the Abbess's remarks and blend their utterances with hers, so that they create a poetic rhythm when they speak. Winifrede is not so astute; she is anxious and clumsy, incurring the impatience of the Abbess. Her failure to allow Alexandra to dictate her every thought betrays a kind of helpless innocence, which the Abbess strongly resents:

If you believe your own ears more than you believe us, Winifrede . . . then perhaps it is time for us to part. It may be you have lost your religious vocation.

Winifrede is regarded with contempt by her superior, who does not hesitate to impute to her all the blame for the untoward goings-on at the convent. Winifrede is very like Mary Macgregor in *The Prime of Miss Jean Brodie*; she cannot quite keep up with what is happening but wants to join in. Her willingness to be used results in the hilarious episode of her meeting with a Jesuit in the Gents in the British Museum in male clothing, to pass on blackmail money. Alexandra's contempt for other nuns does not stop with Winifrede. She sees to it that the junior nuns have cat food to eat, while she and her friends partake of delicacies in the Abbess's parlour.

At the height of her campaign to be elected Abbess, Alexandra delivers a lecture to the other nuns on the aristocratic principles which operated in the convent during the Middle Ages. At this time, there was a pronounced distinction between the *'soeurs nobles'*, those with an aristocratic ancestry, and the daughters of mere tradesmen, the *'soeurs bourgeoises'*. Alexandra appeals to the nuns to perpetuate an aristocratic ethos by being conscious of the state of mind a Lady should maintain. Examples drawn from her pronouncements show very clearly how she understands this elevated state of mind and indeed embodies it: 'A Lady may or may not commit the Cardinal Sins: but a Bourgeoise dabbles in low crimes and safe demeanours.' '. . . a Bourgeoise suffers from the miserable common guilty conscience.' 'A Lady may secretly believe in nothing; but a Bourgeoise invariably proclaims her belief, and believes in the wrong things.' The distinction for Alexandra is one of class and her definition of it shows that she considers herself above the demands for humility and repentance which her order might impose. Her sense of her own innate superiority makes her dismissive of moral values:

Our topics are not those of sanctity and holiness, which rest with God; it is a question of whether you are ladies or not, and that *is* something we decide.

Alexandra's assumptions about her intrinsic worth and her right to ignore any need of contrition or humility lead to much ironic comedy in the book. For example, when Winifrede suggests saying grace before the four select senior nuns embark on their wafers and paté, Alexandra states disdainfully: 'Oh, it isn't necessary. There's nothing wrong with *my* food'. Alexandra's aristocratic indifference to conventional propriety is demonstrated by her outspoken phrasing:

> I must say a Jesuit, or any priest for that matter, would be the last man I would myself elect to be laid by. A man who undresses, maybe; but a man who unfrocks, no.

She refers contemptuously to 'the lax and leaky Jesuit who tumbles Felicity', showing that the activities of the young renegade nun do not shock her by their unorthodoxy but only by their bad taste.

The opposition of Felicity to Alexandra constitutes the basic conflict of the book, and generates the action. Felicity has defied authority and has taken a lover. This is not the reason for Alexandra's dislike of her; Felicity represents a different attitude altogether from Alexandra's powerful techniques of mystification. Felicity wants to express her faith through a positive attitude to humanity. Alexandra is disdainful of this approach and remarks sardonically: 'Felicity will never see the point of faith unless it visibly benefits mankind.' Indeed, Felicity's outlook is very reminiscent of the sixties: love is all one needs. She tells her fellow nuns in her sewing room: 'Love . . . is lacking in our community. We are full of prosperity. We prosper. We are materialistic.' However, Felicity is not frivolous: she insists, for example, that the nuns she supervises in the sewing room should remember the rule of St Benedict on the subject of frivolity and gossip:

> 'What are the tools of Good Works?' says the Rule, and the answers include, 'Not to say what is idle or causes laughter.' Of all the clauses of the Rule, this is the one that Felicity decrees to be the least outmoded, the most adapted to the urgency of our times.

Felicity's insistence on the need for love and for a faith which expresses itself through good works, irritates Alexandra. She pours scorn on what she calls Felicity's 'nauseating propaganda'. Her assertion of the need for love and freedom is described as simply a means to attract the younger nuns so that they might vote for her in the election for the new abbess. These concepts have no substance according to Alexandra:

> She's always talking about love and freedom as if these were attributes peculiar to herself. Whereas, in reality, Felicity cannot love. How can she truly love? She's too timid to hate well, let alone love. It takes courage to practise love. And what does she know of freedom? . . . One who has never observed a strict ordering of the heart can never exercise freedom.

However, Alexandra's mystifying axioms do not tackle the basic strength of Felicity's opposition to her. Felicity tells the nuns in the sewing room that she thinks they should follow St Francis, 'who understood total dispossession and love'. Alexandra has been heard to say: 'to hell with St Francis', asserting her preference for 'more interesting neurotics'. It is clear from the accounts of Felicity's anger that Alexandra is wrong in thinking that Felicity cannot hate: she trembles with fury when she sees the delicacies set out for the exclusive consumption of Alexandra and her close nuns, and when she finds that her sewing box – containing the letters of her Jesuit lover – has been broken into, her 'rage all next day shakes her little body to shrieking point'. When Felicity finally leaves the convent, she is ready to expose all the iniquities she has witnessed. Her indictment – a lengthy paragraph containing Thesaurus' definitions of fraud and wrongdoing – appears in the newspapers, directly, if somewhat tautologically, accusing the Abbess.

The Abbess of Crewe is not a detective story and the plot itself is hilarious, but obscure. The focal point of the satire is the way in which the abbey is run; it is portrayed as entirely out of harmony with any reasonable or even accessible concept. In one of the rare narrative interventions, it is observed how other Benedictine monks and nuns have been 'too lady-like to

protest against how the Lady Abbess ignores the latest reforms
. . . rules her house as if the Vatican Council had never been
. . .'. Indeed, Alexandra is utterly conservative in her insistence
on the following of the offices, even though she herself chants
English poetry to its rhythms. Her convent is feudal in its
class division, the select companions of Alexandra towering
above the other nuns in aristocratic isolation. The other nuns,
relegated to menial tasks and eating cat food, are regarded by
the Abbess with total contempt. Alexandra herself presides over
the presentation of the truth, gifted with a rhetorical grace which
elegantly obscures all that is inconvenient to her. She publicly
declaims that 'history doesn't work':

> Here, in the Abbey of Crewe, we have discarded history. We
> have entered the sphere, dear Sisters, of mythology. My nuns
> love it. Who doesn't yearn to be part of a myth at whatever
> the price in comfort?

So Alexandra insists that the nuns get up twice in the middle
of the night to sing matins and lauds. She insists on the cult
of self-denigration amongst the junior nuns. But in a startlingly
modern way, she has developed an elaborate bugging system,
to keep track of all that is said in her convent, thus ensuring
her power. She claims that this system is no more devious
than steaming open the nuns' letters, and other practices which
have traditionally denied them any independence or liberty. The
nuns are well versed in the workings of these electronic devices,
which they help to run, assuming that their sole purpose is to
maintain contact with Sister Gertrude, a missionary in Africa.
At mealtimes the rules about running these 'devices fearfully
and wonderfully beyond the reach of any humane vocabulary'
are read to them after the Rule of St Benedict and readings
from the Scriptures. Stupidly, the nuns assimilate all. When the
Abbess is demanded by Rome to explain the apparent paradox
between the rigorous observation of demoded practices and the
incorporation of electronic devices, Alexandra sets forth:

That Religion is founded on principles of Paradox. That Paradox is to be accepted and presents no problem. That electronic surveillance ... does not differ from any other type of watchfulness, the which is a necessity of a Religious Community; we are told in the Scriptures to 'watch and to pray' which is in itself a paradox since the two activities cannot be practised together except in the paradoxical sense ...

Alexandra finds no difficulty in justifying her incongruous way of running the convent. Her plot against Felicity to damage her in the eyes of the other nuns she orchestrates in an aloof manner, leaving her close nuns to run her campaign to be elected abbess. Alexandra is preoccupied by her own superiority and by what she calls 'her destiny'. At the same time as she denounces the influence of Felicity over the younger nuns and does her best to ensure Felicity's downfall, Alexandra declares that to be elected abbess is her destiny. Alexandra's destiny is of the same stuff as the mythology she insists should shroud the lives of the nuns; she resents any factual interference into it:

> Walburga says sharply, 'This morning the polls put her (Felicity) at forty-two per cent according to my intelligence reports.'
> 'It's quite alarming', says Alexandra, 'seeing that to be the Abbess of Crewe is my destiny.'

That Alexandra can perpetuate the myth she establishes about herself is an indication of the irrelevance of truth to the life of the convent. Her axiom: 'A lady is free, but a bourgeoise is never free from the desire for freedom', indicates how she considers herself to be wholly untroubled by demands of her fellows or her religion. Towards the end of the book, she states: 'I am become an object of art.' Basically, her mind is aesthetic and she is to herself the object of her principal pleasure and delight, her love of English poetry amplifying the resonances of her sensibility. Her statements about her 'destiny' show how remote her mind is from a view consistent with the Roman Catholic theology of free will. It is pointed out that the nuns in the sewing room go there 'of their free will'. Alexandra worships herself alone; she claims that her mother's pain in giving birth to her was useless if she does not fulfil her destiny. Her lack of any acquiescence before a power beyond her own existence in effect makes her absurd. She plays at God, using her capacity to construct aphorisms to set her seal on her own version of the truth, a version which is intrinsically evil because it is so selfish. Felicity is distressed at the raid on her sewing box, Alexandra – secretly glorying in the diminishment of support for Felicity's election – keeps overtly cool, commenting 'The nasty little bitch can't stand our gentleness.' Her bogus piety is nauseating: 'It is beautiful to be gentle to those who suffer,' she says, in the midst of her campaign to undermine her rival.

The mixture of old-fashioned adherence to the order of autocratic rule over the nuns, of bugging the convent with sophisticated electronic equipment and, eventually, a close study of Machiavelli's counsel on how to maintain power, appear totally incongruous. However, this strange and surrealist way of proceeding demonstrates the consequences of neglect of the principles of Christianity: love and humility. Alexandra has discarded such inconvenient habits. She relished the old order because its lack of openness, its stifling restrictions on individual freedom, act as a screen to allow her to practise her cult of self-adoration. The age-old evils of the monastic system are not at odds with the sophistication of modern technology; both are soulless. *The Abbess of Crewe* may at first sight read like a hilarious farce of convent life and quite possibly, it may appear lacking in all Christian content. One writer has claimed that Muriel Spark 'indulgently treats' Alexandra, that she 'implicitly grants approval to her activities'. It is true that the narrative stresses the character's beauty and dignity, but on a moral level she is sinister. Her mixture of steely lucidity, heartlessness and rhetorical virtuosity isolate her from any sense of common humanity. Of course, Muriel Spark's clearly expressed contempt of the servile nuns can be taken to imply that, personally, she prefers Alexandra's satanic anarchy. Certainly she makes the latter more attractive. Her condemnation of the nuns is blatant:

> A less edifying crowd of human life it would be difficult to find; either they have become so or they always were so; at any rate, they are in fact a very poor lot, all the more since they do not think so for a moment ... They raise to their frightful little lips the steaming beakers of water and they sip as if fancying they are partaking of the warm sap of human experience, ripe for Felicity's liberation.

This indictment of the stupid, unenlightened nuns is as trenchant as Alexandra's quotation from Milton, who condemned the enclosed order for, one assumes, the same reasons as Muriel Spark:

> I cannot praise a fugitive and cloistered virtue, unexercised and unbreathed, that never sallies out and sees her adversary, but slinks out of the race.

Alexandra's borrowing of this observation forms part of her pretended sympathy towards Felicity; in the context of the novel, it is sheer hypocrisy, but it stands out in the moral polarities of the work as a point of reference in its own right.

Muriel Spark intervenes but little to establish a perspective that throws light on the madness of the Abbey of Crewe; the incongruity provokes sufficient laughter for us to be aware of the ironies of the narrative, and irony has no need to be explicit. However, perhaps the ultimate irony is contained in the reading from the Scriptures, which the nuns obediently recite and hear during their mealtimes, but which clearly has no meaning for them at all.

The many quotations from the Scriptures have a moral content which throws sharply into relief the selfish machinations of

Alexandra. One excellent example is the verse from Ecclesiastes which Winifrede obediently and uncomprehendingly reads aloud to the nuns at table:

> Fools are cheated by vain hopes, buoyed up with the fancies of a dream. Wouldst thou heed such lying visions? Better clutch at shadows or chase the wind. Nought thou seest in a dream but symbols; man is but face to face with his own image. As well may foul thing cleanse, as false thing give thee a true warning.

Implied in all readings from the Scriptures are Alexandra's falsity, and the mindlessness of the nuns; the truth of the words from the Bible shows their lack of substance.

Alexandra is characterized in a way which makes her essentially unknowable; she is elegant and static, controlling her nuns as powerfully as she controls her rhetoric. She never shows deference to a power beyond herself although the last lines of the book suggest that she is at last aware of a dimension beyond her. She stands on the ship's deck as it carries her towards Rome:

> . . . marvelling how the wide sea billows from shore to shore like that cornfield of sublimity which never should be reaped nor was ever sown, orient and immortal wheat.

Alexandra's power lies in her ability to mystify. This is made possible for her by certain traditions in the cloistered orders which demand acquiescence. Muriel Spark takes to extreme lengths the absurdity of the Abbess's machinations. However, the evil of her ways emerges clearly: she is selfish, arrogant, contemptuous of others and considers herself beyond any need of restriction or control. Her egocentricity is totally at odds with any understanding of Christianity, the principles of which – love, humility and forgiveness – she rejects out of hand. She is characterized in a way that removes her from the reader; we never see into her mind. She is an order to herself, and thus lacking in humanity.

Selina Redwood: *The Girls of Slender Means*

A first reading of *The Girls of Slender Means* would not, until the end, reveal the devastating power of Selina Redwood. She is notable because of her attractive, slim body, and she impresses the other girls by her dedication to the cult of poise. It is largely the way in which Muriel Spark presents the atmosphere of the hostel in which the girls live that blurs the edges of any latent threat in Selina's personality; her beauty and her selfishness are easily accommodated in this affable although immature community. The events of the novel serve to draw out a latent evil which has far-reaching effects. Her power is initially invisible, both to the characters around her and to the reader.

Unlike many of her other novels, in which Muriel Spark lends the third person narrator a tone which is often distant and almost always ostensibly detached, the narrator of *The Girls of Slender Means* shows a deep warmth towards her characters. This warmth appears to be generated by the individual personalities of these girls living in a hostel in Kensington towards the end of the war. It also stems from the ethos that they unwittingly create. 'Few people alive at the time were more delightful, more savage than the girls of slender means.' These young girls were poor only in the way that middle-class people everywhere in the country were impoverished by the war. But their spirit and their youth were able to transcend the problems of poverty and the menace of wartime conditions, enabling them to create a world of their own, which had its own priorities. One of the visitors to the May of Teck club, a publisher's wife, says that she loves the May of Teck because it reminds her of being back at school.

Indeed, the way the characters are presented at the opening of the book is reminiscent of a story for schoolgirls; they are each described physically and in terms of their individual quirks. We are told of Joanna Childe, a country vicar's daughter, who teaches elocution in her room on the top floor of the May of Teck. Her voice, intoning poetry, floats through the house as she recites for her pupils the verses of which she is so passionately fond; the other girls are 'all very proud of Joanna'. We are briefly told too that Joanna had been in love with one of her father's curates; this had come to nothing but another curate succeeded him in her father's parish, and Joanna felt equally, if not more drawn towards him. Horrified at her own inconsistency, she did her best to suppress this feeling and would not allow herself to be involved with him. Now she gives herself utterly to the poetry through which she teaches her classes. Another cameo picture is given of Pauline Fox, a more mysterious top-floor girl who, every evening, puts on a long dress and disappears, returning to say she has been dining with Jack Buchanan. Jane Wright is a more homely character; she is fat and wrestles constantly with temptation to eat the little pieces of chocolate she has managed to salvage and hide in her cupboard. She does however have 'intellectual glamour' as the other girls call it. She works for a publisher and also spends much time preoccupied with what she calls 'brainwork'. We later find out that this largely involves writing letters to famous writers in the name of some invented character who is calculated to appeal to each; this project is designed to exact a reply with a personal signature. This activity has not been devised by Jane but by her friend, Rudi, to whom she is scrupulously loyal. Jane enjoys being on the fringe of an intellectual world, although in the back of her mind she is intent on looking for a husband. Another of the top-floor girls is Selina Redwood, exceedingly beautiful and slim enough to squeeze through the window in the lavatory on to the flat roof, where one could sunbathe.

These young women, portrayed with charm and economy, arouse the reader's interest and indulgence. However, Spark mentions in her description of them that something savage might well be found in their more endearing qualities. Indeed the events of the narrative lead to a point where moral identities are polarized and the book, instead of being an account of the life of gay young things, reveals deeper spiritual proportions.

The narrative opens with a description of wartime Kensington and relates how the girls of slender means looked out of their windows from the May of Teck club, their eyes 'giving out an eager-spirited light'; this was not genius but youth merely, Spark observes, but the intensity of their lives is clear. In one of her rapid disjunctions of time, Spark proceeds within two pages to recount a telephone conversation between Jane Wright, referred to as 'the woman columnist', and the owner of a model agency; these women turn out to be former members of the May of Teck club, now well established in their professional or domestic lives. Jane Wright asks the other woman if she remembers Nicholas Farringdon who used to go out on to the roof to sleep with Selina in their May of Teck days . . . he has been martyred in Haiti, Jane says.

The reader is then flung backwards into earlier days. After an account of the climate and personalities in the May of Teck, the character to whom Jane Wright refers at the beginning is introduced. He is Nicholas Farringdon. Jane has met him through the publisher for whom she works. He is considered to be one of her 'more presentable' friends, shy and good-looking, 'feeling his way' and reputedly writing something. Jane has instructions from her boss to weigh up Nicholas; to George, the publisher, authors are 'temperamental raw material'. Jane is to investigate Nicholas's work in order to identify the area of which he is most proud. This 'detective work' enables George to find out where the author is most vulnerable; he then has control over him. Nicholas has written a book called the *Sabbath Notebooks* which has already been rejected by ten publishers. George senses that there might be some reason to express interest in this work, but he personally doesn't understand it. He leaves it to Jane to assess its potential. Jane takes on this task in a level-headed manner, but basically it is Nicholas's social charm that interests her more than his intellectual aspirations. She proudly takes him to meet the girls at the May of Teck.

From this point onwards, the May of Teck and its residents are shown through Nick's eyes. He is immediately affected by his encounter with them. He receives from the club a 'poetic image' which stays in his mind – it is a microcosm of an ideal society to him – built on 'beautiful, needless poverty'. Nicholas is reputed to be an anarchist; Jane's friend Rudi tells her that he had passionate relationships with both sexes. He was a pacifist until the war and then the war brought him peace, as he says, and he joined the army. Before this he was drawn towards suicide. This reputation he has acquired through the impressions gleaned by his friends makes him appear eccentric. However, it soon emerges that Nicholas is a serious thinker, trying his best to make some sense of his understanding of life. Rudi reads out to Jane some excerpts from Nick's book; he is himself full of scorn and calls it mediocre. But the excerpts are illuminating; Nick writes, for example, that it is impossible to write a history of anarchism; anarchism is closer to the heartbeat than to political history; analysis would describe its effects but give no account of its intrinsic reality. Nicholas Farringdon is trying to find a way of discussing the realities of society without analysing it in political terms; humanity defies labelling: 'Every communist has a fascist frown; every fascist has a communist smile.'

Rudi isolates parts of Nicholas's text which he declares to be signs of Nick's incipient Catholicism; quite inconsistent with anarchism, he claims. Nick writes that the world has 'so far fallen from grace' that politicians have been appointed keepers of emotions. He thinks that the basic realities of human existence are swept aside to give way to meaningless political cyphers. With little drawn from the *Sabbath Notebooks*, it is clear that Nicholas has a passionate interest in the fabric of society but that he insists on seeing this fabric in terms of human emotional reactions. His attraction to the May of Teck links fundamentally with these views; here he witnesses the existence of people in specific circumstances in an institution without power where they are led by their hearts alone. Such a local structure is what he posits as ideal in his *Notebooks*. Nicholas's ideas are intense but immature; it will take experience to lead him to an understanding of his identity. This experience comes to him in the course of his involvement with the girls of the May of Teck.

Nicholas is fond of Jane; he takes her to poetry readings, where the men read their poems and the women sleep with the men. Nick is unimpressed by this circle; he remarks disdainfully that he can tell when he is in a communist household by the bottles of remedies against dyspepsia on the bathroom shelf. But Jane is entranced. To Nick to take her out is a small return for the excitement and pleasure he derives from his visits to the May of Teck. He wants to know about all the top-floor girls, but especially about Joanna, the elocution teacher, and Selina. Selina, 'furled like a long soft sash' in her chair, captivates Nicholas. He asks Jane to tell him about her. He is particularly struck by Selina's self-imposed habit of repeating two sentences drawn from her 'Poise Course' night and morning. All the girls of the May of Teck are respectfully silent when they hear Selina repeat the sentences. These assert the importance of self-confidence, of 'complete composure' and immaculate grooming whatever the social scene. Selina says these sentences with the devotion and regularity of prayer. In the outcome of later events, this has a particular irony.

Nicholas and Selina have an affair. His mind romantically full of the graceful attributes of common poverty which to him characterize the girls of the May of Teck, he alights on Selina's beauty. She accompanies him on a summer evening dressed in the elegant Schiaparelli gown which the girls share: he says he has never seen such a beautiful dress. Selina represents for Nick all the verve and independence he so much relishes in the girls of the May of Teck. He is aware that his enthusiasm transcends much of the reality of their situation, he admits to himself that he is imposing an image on their society 'incomprehensible to itself'. But, immature and passionate as he is, this paradox suits him. Nonetheless the reader can see that he is so enamoured of the image he has himself devised that he is dangerously unaware of the truth. The narrator's description of Selina's mind shows that it is quite remote from Nick's passionate response to her. When he speaks earnestly of his opinion that central government should be abolished, Selina 'laughs with poise'. She has no interest in his views, but she realizes that they are unorthodox and therefore imply a weakness, a vulnerability in him. Apparently Selina is attracted to men who have both charm and vulnerability; such men do not have the confidence to attempt to possess her entirely. When she recognizes Nick's vulnerability, we are told that Selina thinks she can 'use' him. This intention reveals how self-centred her relationships with others are, and how what she feels for Nick is merely the interest she would have in an accessory to her clothes, or in an agent in social climbing. She is later described sitting on the edge of Nick's bed, giving from under her lashes a disdainful look at his lodgings; such a way of glancing sideways apparently gave her a sense of power. Whilst she only speaks dismissively of his digs and privately longs only for a packet of hair grips, Nicholas pours out his ideas about society to her, striving to awake in her some response to the questions which continually beset his mind. His desire for her is coupled with the urge to make her see the importance of these things. Because her body was 'austere and economically furnished', he feels she should have some intuitive understanding of the moral qualities of the working classes. But she remains unmoved and tells him he sounds funny. Nicholas is not offended; he laughs and agrees with her, anxious to spare her feelings, and not to assert himself. The relationship between Nick and Selina, he obsessed by his preoccupation with social and moral concerns, she, beautiful but insensitive, could have fizzled out as just one of the occasional affairs of wartime Britain. Apparently it had no future, it had no content. However, the climax of the novel reveals a fundamental moral polarity which is to drive an essential truth home into Nick's mind, and to effect his conversion to Catholicism.

When the unexploded bomb goes off, removing a large part of the May of Teck, the narration is low key. The girls' first reaction is to laugh, especially when the plump publisher's wife, who had been stuck in the narrow access to the roof, is suddenly released. But the bomb has severed a gas main, and a fire is creeping slowly into the house. The top half of the fire escape has collapsed. The firemen direct the girls in the house towards the top storey; their aim is to rescue them from the roof. However, until the skylight in the roof is unblocked, the only way to reach the roof is through the narrow window in the lavatory. The girls have in the recent past been very conscious of which of them could or could not squeeze through this opening; it has become desirable and fashionable amongst them to sunbathe on the roof. Selina, moreover, had met Nick out there and slept with him under the stars. Those girls who are able now emerge from the window, some of them injuring themselves in the process. But others, including the pregnant Dorothy Markham and the heavy-boned Joanna, know that for them it is an impossibility. All they can do is wait for the firemen to hack away at the bricks blocking the skylight. This is an ordeal as the smoke begins to creep up the stairs. But Joanna, surrounded by the girls too big to effect an exit, begins to chant the evening's office, the verses and response coming from her lips as the smoke and noise of demolition fill the air. Nick can see her from the roof through the little window, her face streaming with sweat as the heat from the fire mounts. Selina had, of course, been able to emerge from the window without difficulty; Nick had even been fleetingly impressed by her action in handing the blankets he and she had kept on the roof to the girls who had been forced to strip in order to squeeze through the window. But, astonishingly, Selina goes back through the window into the burning house. She passes the little group of anxious girls listening to Joanna, waiting in suppressed panic for the firemen to release them, and goes to fetch something. She carries this object out carefully through the window. It is the Schiaparelli dress. On seeing her bring this out, Nicholas involuntarily makes the sign of the cross: this is his response to what Spark in an earlier paragraph, anticipating the event, calls an 'act of savagery so extreme'.

Joanna Childe is killed in the fire. Her strong moral qualities are highlighted in retrospect as a result. Jane Wright had envied her ability to forget herself and her personality; in the fire her calm and courage as she rhythmically repeated the evening's office show that, as Nicholas is later to tell her father, she had religious strength. Nicholas goes into the Church and becomes a missionary priest. He had written in the *Sabbath Notebooks*: 'A vision of evil can be as effective to a conversion as a vision of good.' The consequence of his conversion, as we know from the beginning of the book where Jane spreads the news amongst her former friends from May of Teck days, is that he is martyred in Haiti. He had always said he would be famous but was ignorant of the hideous way in which his hopes would be fulfilled. Yet in the terms of his faith, such a death would mean a triumph. It was an achievement of which he could have been proud in a world where the polarities of good and evil had been strikingly brought home to him. His martyrdom was a triumph over the power of evil which he had witnessed in this microcosm of a society he had thought to be ideal.

Selina's power is retrospectively chilling. Her attractive appearance has lured Nicholas, to the point where he is quite unaware of the limitations of her mind and – paradoxically – regards her as an image of the community of the May of Teck. He is deceived by her and also by his own romanticism. But the fire and the events which it instigates bring home to him the realities he has hitherto been able to ignore. Not only is Selina unable and unwilling to follow his intellectual arguments, she has no compassion. The fellow-feeling in which Nicholas delighted when he identified in the May of Teck girls an ideal community redolent of the graceful attributes of common poverty, is quite absent in Selina. Her action in stepping past the trapped girls in the midst of the fire in order to steal the Schiaparelli dress gives Nicholas an insight into an evil he has never fully reckoned with.

He says himself in his *Sabbath Notebooks* that an evil act

can have a positive effect, and in this case his conversion and subsequently his martyrdom turn out to be that effect. In Nicholas's own life the power of evil has been exorcized. But the narrative does not confine its detection of evil merely to Selina. In the midst of the VJ crowd Nicholas perceives a seaman drawing out a knife and stabbing a woman between the ribs; she sags and falls silently to the ground. Nicholas tries in vain to draw attention to what has happened. In the text of the book it is stated: He did this for no apparent reason and to effect, except that it was a gesture. As the letter was the result of a complicit fraudulence between himself and Jane, it could be understood as a tacit admission of his own sinfulness.

Nicholas now is aware of the ubiquitous presence of evil, but the enduring image he retains until his death is that of plump Jane, pinning up her straggling hair in the crowds, sturdy and resilient. Although he had been deceived and seduced by Selina, his recognition of the spirit of humanity amongst the girls was a genuine perception of moral worth.

Maggie Radcliffe: *The Takeover*

It is perhaps unfair to call Maggie Radcliffe a woman of power. She is extremely rich and a number of people are dependent on her. Her identity derives basically from her wealth, and her consequent ability to lead a luxurious and glamorous existence. She attracts men to the point of making their heads swim. However, it emerges in the narrative that wealth has no substantial power. Indeed the nature of any power is questioned and shown to be riddled with deception. Maggie's personality is unstable as a result of the pressures brought about by her wealth. She ultimately finds ways of eluding those who seek to rob her. But at no time does she manifest any spiritual or moral resources which lend her a status rising above the nefarious activities which threaten her financial stability.

It is essential to Muriel Spark's purpose in this book that Maggie appear both vulnerable and yet overbearing. Much of the text is given to description of the beauty of the landscape at Nemi where Maggie has three houses. The loveliness of Italy in the spring and the elegance of the life led by Maggie's son and daughter-in-law combine to form an image of *la dolce vita* as seductive and apparently as enduring as Maggie herself. We are told that Maggie's age is irrelevant to her power to attract; she needs still to have people's attention focused on her and this she achieves in an imperious way. She 'overdressed tastefully', knowing exactly how to judge the demands of the society in which she moves. However, she is not a mere glossy magazine prototype: we are shown that she takes a genuine interest in what is going on around her. But she doesn't think much further, nor more deeply. She makes sweeping statements, calling, for example, the secretary of her tenant, Hubert, a 'penniless Lesbian' when she has never met her. She clearly sees her role as being judgmental and absolute.

There are, however chinks in her armour. She is constantly preoccupied with the difficulty in persuading the tenant of her house in Nemi, Hubert, to move out. She is aware of the limits of her power in this case and spends much time and energy deprecating the situation. Hubert was a friend of hers in earlier days and she was fascinated by his familiarity with artistic circles. She had allowed him to influence her and it was with his consultation that she had bought her houses at Nemi. However, she has long since ceased to be impressed by him and is now beginning to feel alarm at his apparently limitless occupancy of her house. Many times in the narrative she declares passionately that she hates him, at one point so intensely that her tone causes both her husband and her lover to feel jealous. Hubert on the other hand, knows Maggie well and has perhaps a more accurate perception of her than anyone else in the narrative. He says of a letter she sends him suggesting he depart from her house:

She has an epistolary style which denotes an hysterical need for stability and order. In conversation she counts on her remarkable appearance to hypnotize the immediate environment into a kind of harmony.

True as this observation might be, Maggie is uncalculating about her ability to create this impact, which she does quite intuitively. Maggie has little self-control. At the news of the theft of her jewellery when in their summer house, she has hysterics and needs much soothing from her husband to calm down. She accuses someone present at random. Her husband, Berto, an Italian marchese, is ideal for her since he accords her all the little attentions she likes. When she thinks that her picture by Gauguin has been stolen, she is 'sweetly mellowed by the fragrant distillations of Berto's talk'. For all his charm and courtesy, however, she confesses to being bored by him in bed. She is sexually far more responsive to Lauro, the Italian boy who is part servant, part secretary to her son.

Maggie is imperilled by her riches and throughout the narrative we are told of plots to rob her. Hubert, the tenant of her house in Nemi, has for a long time been ensuring his own financial security by having Maggie's furniture and paintings copied, replacing the originals with these copies and then selling the originals. The irony of this subterfuge lies in the fact that Maggie trusts Hubert utterly with the care of her works of art and her furniture. Whilst avowing that he is himself 'sheer fake', she has no idea that her chairs and her pictures are rapidly becoming the same. Hubert's treacherous handling of her property is portrayed as quite a predictable and understandable venture; he knows Maggie wants him to leave the house and he tells himself that he is merely making provision for his eventual impoverishment. Lauro too is unworried by the idea of robbing his employer. When Maggie gives him some ancient coins to deliver secretly to Hubert so that he will not be totally destitute, Lauro has no compunction in appropriating half of them and burying them next to his mother's grave.

Wealth is shown to be inevitably susceptible to predators but this predatory factor does not necessarily undermine personal feelings. Lauro finds Maggie very attractive and is happy to be her lover. Hubert retains a profound fondness for Maggie and at one moment longs desperately to ring her. Berto, Maggie's husband, is touched by the visit to his villa of self-proclaimed art historians even though the genuine reason for their interest in his property is to rob it; emotional vulnerability and financial vulnerability go hand in hand.

This is a world in which it is no longer safe to be rich; it is the end of 1973 when, as Muriel Spark points out in the narrative, there is a 'change in the meaning of property and money'. Assets rapidly became liabilities; the more they were changed into mere figures, the more possible it was for fraud to take place. It is through her devious financial adviser, Coco de Renault, that Maggie eventually loses all her money. However, despite material instability of this privileged social climate, there is a far more dangerous and insidious threat. The theme of deception and fraud on a spiritual level develops side by side with that of preoccupation with material possession. It is seen to be far more difficult to counter.

Hubert Mallindaine claims to be a direct descendant of the goddess Diana to whom the groves of Nemi were once sacred. In persuading Maggie to buy land on this site Hubert had been able to indulge his fascination with the cult of Diana. His claims to this divine ancestry appear eccentric, suspect and self-indulgent. The reader is told that they derive from nothing more than a tale spread by two of Hubert's maiden aunts: inspired by Sir James Frazer's study of comparative religion, *The Golden Bough*, they connived with some late Victorian genealogists to establish an etymology of the name Mallindaine, proving that the family were descendants of Diana and the Emperor Caligula. Hubert had taken up this fantasy with relish, identifying powerfully with the beauties of the landscape around Nemi. When some remains of the temple to Diana are discovered in the woodlands nearby, Hubert is ecstatic and calls out that he is king of Nemi and that the place is his. 'And whether he was sincere or not; or whether he was or was not connected so far back as the divinity-crazed Caligula . . . at any rate these were the words that Hubert cried.'

The dimensions of sincerity and truth are in fact very far from Hubert's mentality. His cult, which has grown rapidly in the area from 1974, is based on the worship of Diana as it was before Christianity replaced her with Mary. Hubert expounds a theology allegedly founded on spiritual values and decrying material wealth; he points to inflation and the collapse of the economy in Europe as proof of the corruption of materialism. In the world of symbolism, mysticism and magic such decadence does not exist, he claims; there is no place for lies and fraud. It is very clear to the reader how phoney Hubert's sermon is; his exploitation of Maggie's property is a classic example of fraud. Hubert's secretary, Pauline Thin, interrupts one of his vast gatherings with a reference to the Scriptures which throws Hubert's self-indulgent, deceptive theology into perspective. Although until now her Catholicism has played little part in the narrative, Pauline's decision to quote publicly words from the Scriptures denouncing the cult of the Goddess Diana and her magnificence cuts cleanly through Hubert's histrionic mystification.

It is pointed out in the narrative how the heady atmosphere induced in Hubert's gatherings is similar to the religiosity of the charismatic movement which at that time was taking hold in the Roman Catholic Church. Hubert pores over a newspaper describing a meeting of the Charismatic Renewal Movement in Rome; it is characterized by fervent prayer meetings, recounts the newspaper, gifts of the spirit such as speaking in tongues and efforts to breathe new life into personal religion. Pauline Thin tells Hubert about one such meeting she has herself attended; she says that although there was a mass, it only preceded the meeting, the substance of which was singing, dancing and kissing. Hubert excitedly refers to it as an orgy. The fallacy of the 'personal religion' identified both in the charismatic movement here and also in Hubert Mallindaine's cult, emerges very clearly as a form of self-indulgence in which subjective emotional appetite is gratified and there is no discipline of humility or penitence. Spark comments on Hubert's prayer to Diana, saying that he took the nature of prayer as an intimate form of contact which would ensure the fulfilment of any wish that passed through his mind. Spark adds archly that he made this mistake in common with ministers of other religions.

This is a morally bleak novel since neither of the challenges it describes is met. That of the instability of wealth and that of mystification wrought by emotive and selfish religious mania are seen to hold indomitable sway. Maggie is sufficiently crafty to think of a way to counter her fraudulent financial adviser; she has him kidnapped. She also arranges rather less successfully to have Hubert assassinated. It is clear that Maggie's wealth will never be safe, nor despite her resilience and resourcefulness will she be safe from threats to it. As she stays, her only way of countering those in league against her is to become criminal herself. Material possessions are shown to have no substance; by some quirk of Italian law, Maggie is found not to possess the land on which her houses stand at all. Hubert, however, appears to have more substantial prospects since he is taking up the charismatic movement in the Roman Catholic Church and is to run their prayer meetings.

Wealth is shown to have sufficient power to create a highly desirable lifestyle, and indeed to have created Maggie's seductive personality. She is not obsessed by wealth, rather she takes it for granted as she takes for granted the loyalty and support of her friends and relatives. However, it is clear to the reader that Maggie's wealth makes her a focal point in the lives of all her dependents and also that it draws towards her horrific threats of insecurity.

The irony of the book lies in the ascendancy of Hubert's power. He has no money; indeed, he is a crook. But the devious way in which he develops his eccentric cult of Diana shows that he has power over minds. Criminality in terms of possessions appears far less harmful. Although the success of Hubert's cult might merely seem laughable, the sinister element in it is implied by the way in which Spark associates it with the highly successful charismatic movement in the Catholic Church.

Margaret Murchie: *Symposium*

The narrative technique of Muriel Spark's most recent novel, *Symposium*, is beguiling. This book invites the reader to contribute fully to its impact. The reader perceives the issues at stake as the characters, at an equal pace, discover these issues themselves. The development of *Symposium* is gentle, but artfully economical; the copious dialogue is never wasteful but, on the contrary, succeeds both in constructing mood and character, and also in sustaining the momentum of the plot. Little by little we find ourselves in the shadow of the horror and evil which penetrate the lives of a circle of wealthy people, sedate and of good taste. We are as surprised and as disconcerted as they.

The title of the book suggests a good deal; as in the classical symposium people of varying minds met to share their thoughts around a feast, so Spark shows how an artist and an Australian business woman prepare to invite guests to a dinner party. The purpose, however, is exclusively social, although they comment later in the book that they like their guests to be highly intelligent. Because of the circumstances of the novel, all the guests will share an experience of which they are never fully conscious, but which they encounter intuitively. Through the fragmentary perceptions of Hurley, Chris and their guests, and through their sharing of responses, the reader also is able to assemble an experience and a perception.

One of the guests, we slowly discover, is different from the rest: Margaret Damien, née Murchie, is impenetrable to all who meet her. This lack of accessibility to others is puzzling to the reader, who must struggle to piece together what is said about her and what she herself says. Initially Margaret draws the reader's attention but little; later a mystery appears to surround her, later yet, she emerges as untrustworthy, selfish and deliberately evil. The skill of the narrative lies in the development of its portrayal of this complex character.

Throughout *Symposium* we have no insight into Margaret's mind. She first appears at the dinner party itself. This event is the focal point of the narrative and is returned to at several moments. It alone is recounted in the present tense. All preceding events, some of which date back as far as two years, are in the past tense and three brief paragraphs at the end of the book are in the future tense. These changes of tense, together with constant adjustments of the time sequence in the rest of the narrative, make the focus on the dinner party very distinct.

A glimpse of the dinner is one of the earliest sequences in the novel, and at this point an important statement is made in an unusual intervention in the narrative: 'their eight guests are far better known to each other than they are at present to us.' This remark makes the reader conscious of the role there will be to play in the reading of this book; the knowledge and the impressions it imparts will eventually enlighten us. Our first encounter with Margaret is in the impact she makes socially. She is mentioned in the course of a short account of the conversation over the table, in which a general impression of the guests, of their appearance, their manners and their remarks, is given. We are told of the beauty of Margaret's dark red hair; she is romantic-looking, but more startlingly romantic is her sudden bursting out into poetry:

Look thy last on all things lovely,
Every hour.

However, in contrast with this somewhat awesome quotation,

we are made aware of her capacity to make apparently empty-headed remarks: having heard the news that one of their dinner companions was robbed the previous night, she suggests that perhaps there is 'some good in robberies' and adds, sanctimoniously, that some mystics have said that 'to divest yourself of all your possessions is a supreme good'. Roland, her neighbour, points out that there is a difference between divesting oneself of one's goods and being robbed. This is the first indication of how Margaret thinks only of the impresson she is trying to make, rather than trying to communicate.

The narrative then turns back to Margaret's honeymoon in Venice, which was spent a fortnight before. The couple have not known each other long, and William Damien's infatuation with his bride is all too apparent. Through his eyes, we see her in the light of adoration. Above all, he admires her moralistic tendency. She would never criticize anyone, which he finds 'old-fashioned and refreshing'. She even manages to dispel in his mind the smells of Venice, through saying something positive about them. He saw her as being 'on the side of light'. The impression he has of her goodness gives her a mystical aura, and it is credible that he thinks she is about to levitate when they visit the painting of the Assumption in the Ferrari. However, we are made aware too of some misgivings of which he is half conscious; Margaret's insistence that some exalted message should be drawn from fine art is not to his taste; he also finds her apparent high-mindedness beyond him. The reader is startled by her interest in William's job as a researcher into the devising of artificial intelligences; her excitement at this idea seems to conflict with the image she clearly seeks to convey of bestower and reflector of natural goodness and beauty.

When, after their return from honeymoon, Hurley is invited to meet Margaret, his reactions to her make her seem still more incongruous in the mind of the reader. Hurley is bemused that 'she has to drape herself in green against a background of fall foliage'. Her teeth, which have a gap, contrast with her contrived image and he wonders why she does not arrange some cosmetic adjustment; altogether, he finds her odd, an impression which he later imparts to his friend Chris, telling her that he does not think the marriage will last beyond a year. This conviction seems to be the result of his sense of incongruity – and implicitly, untrustworthiness about her. Chris muses that she thinks she has seen Margaret's surname – Murchie – in the papers somewhere, a remark which appears casual at this stage, but which will acquire considerable significance further on in the book. Most importantly, Chris and Hurley identify the hollowness of Margaret's moral pose. He tells her how Margaret, on their first meeting, had mentioned a French philosophy she terms *Les Autres*. Hilda, William's mother, is 'absolutely immersed in it', she tells Hurley. Hurley explains to Chris that Margaret defines *Les Autres* as focusing one's thoughts exclusively on others, neglecting entirely one's own interests. Chris comments that this is something one does naturally anyway, and is annoyed that her old friend Hilda should be described as taking up and practising philosophy; she knows her as a busy, active woman. 'The girl must be mad,' she comments. Intuitively, before meeting Margaret, she has hit on something essential and strange. A rapid leap forward to the dinner party itself at this point shows Hurley, who describes himself as basically a Catholic, talking at length about the unreliability of the state of most people's minds when they contract a marriage. 'Love-passion' is a form of madness, he declares, and therefore does not validate the permanent joining together of a couple. This remark appears to be an airy dinner party gambit, but reflections of what we have been told of William and Margaret's recent marriage, and the apparently besotted state of William's mind, lead us to link Hurley's observations on marriage with what we know of this one. Suddenly, at the end of this short sequence, we learn that Hilda, William's mother, who is expected after dinner for coffee, is at that very moment dying. To be told this casts a shadow over what we have encountered until now as a highly social environment, rich in comfort and contact.

We next are taken back to a fortnight earlier, when we

encounter Hilda, who is speaking to Chris on the telephone. This conversation displays Hilda as a friendly, practical woman. We also learn that she is uneasy about her son's recent marriage; having just met Margaret and her family, who live in St Andrews, she recounts to Chris the 'sensation of oddness' she picked up while she was there. Of Margaret, particularly, she is suspicious. The reader has learned, from what Margaret told Hurley, that she and William had met over the fruit and vegetable counter in Marks and Spencer; this account did not appear to the reader unacceptable when first mentioned in the narrative, but now Hilda questions it. She wants to know why Margaret needed vegetables, when she was staying in a half-board hostel. Her suspicion of Margaret and of the Murchie family is something she can't quite understand, and we are told next of her feeling that there was 'something wrong' at the time of her visit to their house. However, as we are told about her unease, we also learn much about Hilda which contrasts vigorously with this state of mind. She is attractive, self-possessed, and aware of her ability to radiate independence and charm. She asks herself why she should bother about William's 'goody, goody bride'; she dismisses it merely as his 'first marriage'. As for Margaret, she fixes on her a 'best Sandringham-type manner', asking sternly if Marks and Spencer is her favourite fruit shop.

The reader by now has derived several kaleidoscopic impressions of Margaret; to all but William she appears pretentious, sanctimonious and strange; his mother's unease contrasts starkly with William's infatuation, and appears linked to a more fundamental response than dislike for merely social reasons. Although it crosses her mind, Hilda refuses to contemplate seriously the possibility that Margaret is after William's money.

We are now to learn more about Margaret Murchie. After a brief conversation between two more of Hurley and Chris's dinner guests, which takes place a fortnight beforehand, we hear Roland, a genealogist, talking to his cousin Annabel; he says that he had heard of the Murchies; apparently they had claimed a family fortune. He had read this in the papers.

Now we meet the Murchies. The narrative moves backwards two years. They are described in their sitting room, on a glorious October day. Significantly, Margaret introduces a new character: her uncle Magnus. She is asking his advice. Magnus Murchie is to be a major character in the book. He is a character far outside the social coterie which has hitherto been presented to us. The narrator comments: 'Magnus was the only imaginative factor that had occurred in the Murchie family, but unfortunately he was mad.' His former violence had been controlled by modern medicine, but he is still a forceful character. Dan and Greta, Margaret's parents, are convinced he has a privileged insight, Greta remembering how fools were venerated in the Middle Ages.

In response to Margaret's request for advice, Magnus, as their guru, recommends a course of action 'which', the narrator informs us, 'is to cause the Murchie scandal'. He suggests that Dan's elderly and ailing mother, now in a nursing home, should be persuaded to leave all her money to Dan exclusively. She had originally divided her wealth in her will between her five children. Quoting the Bible grandiloquently, Magnus tells them that he does not want his share of the money. Dan is not convinced that he should encourage his mother to change her will in the way Magnus suggests. Two of his sisters, we are told, are unmarried and 'decidedly helpless'.

Dan is surprised and alarmed to find that his mother is almost immediately visited by a lawyer and has arranged to change her will in the way Magnus has suggested. Events move rapidly: Mrs Murchie has a heart attack and then, while in hospital, is strangled – apparently by an escaped maniac.

Greta and Dan immediately have the feeling that Magnus has in some way engineered these happenings. They soon discover that Margaret is indeed indirectly involved. She tells Greta, who rings her at Dan's suggestion, that she had herself arranged for the lawyer to visit her grandmother. She says that old Mrs Murchie had seemed greatly in favour of the new arrangements and was delighted with the flowers Waters the lawyer had brought her, together with a half-drafted new will. 'At least she died happy,' Margaret comments; a somewhat surprising observation about someone who has been strangled to death. Greta and Dan are extremely uneasy. Dan feels he might be going mad. Both are convinced that Magnus is involved in old Mrs Murchie's death; it seemed too great a coincidence that the young psychotic who killed her had escaped from the Jeffrey King Hospital, where Magnus was himself a resident. Dan says to Greta that he would be 'stunned' if he thought Margaret was party to the murder, but Greta replies that she is sure of this. The new circumstances however have led Dan, who has always adored his daughter, to feel estranged from her. When Margaret arrives to see them the day after the murder has been announced, they 'look at her with fear, not quite knowing her for the first time in their lives'.

Margaret's disdain of their suggestion that Uncle Magnus had something to do with the murder is accompanied by her outright refusal to accept any money for herself. She tells Dan that she could not bear to profit from 'darling granny's death'. Although Dan is compelled to agree that they have no proof about Magnus's involvement, still less of Margaret's, the situation clearly puts great strain upon him. He is amazed by the arrival of Margaret's sisters, seeking to loot their grandmother's possessions. He is disturbed by the sight of the wooden box, containing his mother's body. But above all, he is overwhelmed by a deep feeling that it was Margaret who had sent the maniac to his mother. His besotted love for her, in many ways a prelude to William's obsession in years to come, is becoming tainted with fear and dismay. Magnus, on coming to St Andrews, dressed in his usual gaudy clothes, praises Margaret to Dan. Dan dares consult his brother about Margaret's capacity for being responsible for a murder, to which Magnus gives his full assent. He declares that there was nothing she could not do; she is 'a capable girl, full of ability and power'. He sees no disparity between the possibility that she could arrange a murder, and the highmindedness she is showing by refusing to touch any of the grandmother's money. She is 'naturally a girl of high principle', he observes. What Margaret's principles are and how they operate, is becoming increasingly obscure. Dan ponders deeply about Margaret's sanity. 'Perhaps she inherited something wild from me?' Magnus suggests, saying at the same time to his brother, 'My divine affliction is your only guide.' The 'something wild' offered by Margaret and her uncle to illuminate and expedite family affairs is to Dan an increasing source of anxiety.

The narrative briefly moves two years on and we find Chris and Hurley discussing Margaret. Hurley is fascinated by her combination of 'honey and cream philosophy of *Les Autres* and her aggressive teeth. Chris tells him that Hilda suspects Margaret of enticing her son and she observes how potentially wealthy a husband she has acquired. This reads as chit-chat, but there are darker undercurrents for the reader, who has just learned of Margaret's ominous involvement in her grand-mother's death. However, Chris and Hurley as yet know nothing of this. Hurley remarks that if Margaret were after William's inheritance from Hilda, they would have to wait a long time since she was so fit. This short conversation brings the central issues to the mind of the reader: Hurley and Chris's agreement that Margaret is strange, the idea that the meeting between Margaret and William at Marks and Spencer was unlikely enough to have been engineered, and Hilda's eerie and intuitive sense, which she tries to dismiss, that Margaret might be after her money. At this point, nevertheless, there seems to be no imminent threat.

The next sequence returns once more to Margaret's activities two years previously, this time after her grandmother's death. She has joined an Anglican convent where the nuns, somewhat unconvincingly, proclaim a form of neo-Marxism and commit-ment to the Third World. Their unorthodoxy is exemplified by Sister Marrow who swears bluntly and is both crass and heavily impatient. Margaret's unassuming presentation of herself as a novice with the Sisters of Good Hope is a further incongruity in the narrative. She appears to take it all in her stride, telling

103

the novice mistress that she feels 'sent', and fitting in easily
with visits to the sick and the routine of the convent life. She
writes to her father about it, recounting blandly the odd set-up
in the convent, even quoting without apparent embarrassment
the uncouth vocabulary of Sister Marrow. She mentions that
the Mother Superior is ill in bed. 'Such a tragic case,' she
comments.

This letter is the only opportunity the reader has had to
witness the interior of Margaret's mind. But possibly this letter
is designed only for effect. Dan is bewildered by his daughter's
decision to join the nuns, wondering despite himself, 'what she
is up to'. He hopes her involvement with the convent won't last
long; evidently he feels more estranged from his daughter than
ever. Magnus, however, appears to have some clue about his
niece's presence amongst the nuns. He observes that madness
commonly takes the form of religious mania. The Murchies,
he says, were 'Covenanting stock', refusing to accept the rule
of bishops. Margaret might well be under divine orders, he
suggests. He also comments, on hearing of the sickness of the
Mother Superior, that he hopes nothing will happen to the old
lady. Dan realizes that Magnus, in some way, anticipates another
disaster involving his daughter. 'Oh, God. Oh, God,' is all he
can say. He clearly has a sense of helplessness, as if the strange
power in Margaret carries all before it, and he cannot identify
it nor restrain it.

Magnus's anticipation of some disaster happening to the
Mother Superior proves well-founded. However, it is not she
who is murdered, but she who confesses to committing a
murder. The victim is a young nun, Sister Rose, who, in
a recent television programme made about the convent, had
been seen as an assistant to an older nun, skilled in plumbing.
The Mother Superior apparently confesses to the murder quite
freely, and even cites the cause of it: she had been annoyed by
Sister Rose who had asked on the television programme why
the nuns had no spiritual life. Since the Mother Superior had
long been bed-ridden, it was difficult to believe her confession.

The problem is easily shelved shortly afterwards, when the old nun dies of a heart attack, and a book on karate is found in her bedroom. The police doubtfully acquiesce before the statement she had made.

Margaret had spent much time with the Mother Superior; it had been her task to sit by her bedside and keep her company. From the account given of the making of the television programme two months earlier, Margaret treated the other nuns with a disdain bordering on contempt; Sister Marrow comments: 'She's only been here three weeks, and she thinks she fucking well runs the convent.' Also, we read that Margaret hears from the talk of the Mother Superior that one of the nuns has a discarded husband who occasionally visits her, dressed as a curate. We are told that Margaret kept her eyes open for him, but nothing more. However, we are also told that the police found it impossible to tell whether Sister Rose had been strangled by a man or by a woman, but that the killer had large hands. None of the nuns, including the Mother Superior, it is stated, had particularly large hands. The death of Sister Rose remains a mystery. But, now that the text has aroused suspicion of Margaret, it is not a surprise to read in a letter addressed to her father that Uncle Magnus has himself expressed his sense of her involvement in the matter. Margaret states haughtily that she was visiting her sister at the time of the murder and that there was no reason at all to think she had anything to do with it. When faced with this, Magnus quotes Schopenhauer at her: 'chronology is not causality'. The reader can only start to guess at the degree of her participation. By now we are familiar with her arrogance, which lies only slightly below her veneer of religiosity. Sister Rose's demands for a spiritual life might well have triggered irritation above all in Margaret. For some reason, her alibi is inadequate to allay suspicions.

A flash forward to preparations for Hurley and Chris's dinner party shows Margaret and William in their flat; she has put together their collection of woolly toys, impressing William with her sweetness. The reader is less impressed by her reflections on the validity of the practice of sticking pins into dolls to cast a spell. She admits that she would pity the dolls in such circumstances. Once again we are given an insight into her doubtful priorities.

Meanwhile, other elements in the tale are developing. Hilda tells Chris she intends to take the Monet she has bought for William and Margaret to their new flat in Hampstead while the dinner party goes on. Annabel and Roland pool cuttings in the paper about the Murchie murder; Annabel also remembers seeing Margaret in the television programme about the Sisters of Good Hope.

The next journey into the past offers still more information about Margaret. The Murchie sisters recall the 'unfortunate incidents' which occurred in Margaret's schooldays: at twelve she had seen her best friend drown, in circumstances never fully explained. Shortly after this, Margaret was moved discreetly to another school. A schoolteacher who took Margaret out to tea disappeared, having gone to the Ladies from the tearoom. She was never seen again. Her sisters had, since their childhood, been frightened of Margaret. When they hear of the murder at the convent, Margaret's parents are overwhelmed with dread. The sequence of disasters which had occurred when Margaret was nearby were by now too many to dismiss through any kind of common sense. The narrator observes that Greta and Dan might have been to a degree consoled if they could have been assured that there was no link, 'rational, physical or psychological' between what Margaret herself did and the odd events with which they fearfully associated her. The narrator comments that they had 'every reason' to be frightened, even though there were no reasonable terms which could explain their fear.

At this point in the novel, the flashback to events in the Murchie household and the present preparations for the dinner party move closer together. The consequence of this is that for the first time in the narrative, we see clearly human intention behind the sequence of events. Uncle Magnus tells Margaret she should marry. She appreciates his recognition of her independence, and asks him whether he thinks she has 'the evil eye'.

Magnus says that he is quite sure of it and that others have begun
to notice it too. Margaret then makes a revealing statement: she
says that she is tired of being 'the passive carrier of disaster'.
She wants to make disasters come about. When Magnus asks if
she wishes to perpetrate evil, she says she does. 'The wish alone
is evil,' comments Magnus.

From now on, the reader is no longer in any doubt as to
Margaret's identity. Whereas, when told of a time before this
conversation with Magnus, we are invited only to sense intuitively
Margaret's propensity for wickedness, we now perceive how a
new dimension has come into being through her announcement
that she will henceforth deliberately pursue it. We now learn
how, having been selected in a more or less arbitrary way from
a list of rich bachelors, William Damien becomes the object of
Margaret's scheming. We find that, as Hilda Damien suspected,
the encounter in Marks and Spencer was contrived. We see that
Margaret's soulfulness and sweetness are, as Hurley and Chris
had guessed, artificial. William is evidently in a trap.

Margaret again counsels her uncle, who asks her straight away
how she intends to 'get rid' of William's mother. Margaret has
indeed begun to make plans. She states that this is something
different from 'the evil eye'. She calls her intentions 'healthy
criminality'. Magnus, whose mind is steeped in the mythology
of evil and in the Bible, appears to think that the opportunity will
present itself to perpetrate evil, but Margaret insists that planning
is necessary. She thinks an accident would be a good idea and
suggests that when she visits St Andrews Magnus should push
her mother-in-law into the pond. She is now evil in a calculating
way, impatient with Magnus's reservation that success could not
be certain.

By this stage in the narrative, the reader knows more than
the characters do with the exception of Magnus and Margaret.
We are told of Roland and Annabel's discussion on whether to
tell Hurley of what they have pieced together about Margaret's
suspect past. They do so and consequently Hilda is told. She is
not surprised; this information confirms her unease about her

daugher-in-law. Chris's pleas to her to be careful can inevitably have little effect. Hilda does not know how to be careful, nor what to be careful of. She continues to follow through her plan. However, her mind is beset with increasing fear and suspicion. She is convinced that Margaret is plotting against her; she is certain that Margaret in some way knows that she has bought the Monet. This is not the case, but her intuition does advise her well, as far as the reader knows, by prompting her to withdraw from the invitation from Margaret's parents to visit them in St Andrews that weekend.

The ultimate evolution of the story puts Margaret's sinister evil into a different perspective. In the end, it is not Margaret's evil eye, nor her plotting that brings about Hilda's death. From the beginning of the novel, another level of crime has been recounted, starting with the robbery of Lord Suzy. Throughout the book, it emerges that the butler, Charterhouse, Corbey the cook, and Luke, an attractive student who helps Ernst and Ella, two more of the dinner party guests, are in league. Luke, it is said, has acquired gifts which Ella and Ernst suspect to be rewards for sexual favours. In fact, it emerges that Luke's advice on which houses are left unguarded and where valuable property is left, proves to be singularly convenient to this gang of thieves. Luke has been able to inform them about the Monet in the Hampstead flat. Hilda's decision to take the painting to the flat herself is something about which the thieves have not been informed; since they are recognizable to her, they kill her. The result is that Margaret's power is thwarted. When she hears of Hilda's death, she loses all self-control. She cries out: 'It shouldn't have been till Sunday.' The failure of her power strikes her more forcefully than any concern for the impression she makes. She realizes that her evil eye is impotent.

The reader might well wonder by the end of this book why the sinister character of Margaret has been so much its focal point. Every murder which occurs appears in some way linked with her, although there is no evidence whatsoever. Finally, when she is known to have planned a murder, her plans come to nothing.

But *Symposium* is not a detective story, and so to look for patterns of such a kind is fruitless. It is the work of a moralist, and it is in this area that we learn so much. The power of Margaret Murchie is awesome because she has the capacity to manipulate people. Unlike the other characters in this book, she is not of a mind that can be opened to the reader. Yet subtly her character is implied by her effect on others.

A principal feature of Margaret's character is her religiosity. Her readiness to moralize is apparent at every stage in the book and, ironically, William is most enamoured of this trait. Seen from other perspectives, we find that Margaret's sanctimonious observations induce nausea. Her constant references to the spurious philosophy of *Les Autres* show her as academically as well as morally pretentious; Chris dismisses her claims succinctly when she says that, quite spontaneously, one puts the needs of others before one's own. Increasingly during the narrative Margaret's pose strikes the reader as artificial: her refusal to benefit from 'darling granny's death' carries no weight, since we have seen for ourselves how ready Margaret was to dupe her. When Margaret talks of her visit to her sister, expressing great affection for her nephew, she later refers to him as a 'squalling brat'. Most revealing, however, is the way she speaks to Magnus of Hilda. She calls her 'very limited' and a 'know-all'. She also says that Hilda is 'comparatively stingy'. From someone who has just been given a flat in Hampstead, this comment sounds amazing. Margaret is clearly pleased that she did not like Hilda: we identify the ill will that Hilda has sensed since she met Margaret. When Margaret starts to lay plans to murder Hilda, she tells Magnus that she wishes to feel guilty for 'a real case of guilt'. Magnus tells her that she is more likely to feel exalted, to gloat on her achievement: she is content at this prospect.

As the book progresses, a fundamental selfishness, an indifference to others and a pretentiousness emerge: all of these lead Margaret to use people and to deceive them. More than the information given objectively to the reader, the response of other characters to Margaret shapes our reactions. Hurley's first feelings about her are telling. He realizes that her dress is pretentious, and observes the aggression in her protruding teeth. He and Chris find Margaret unnatural, as indeed she appears increasingly to her parents. Their horror at their daughter, without knowing the cause, is another intuitive perception. Above all, Hilda's deepening mistrust of Margaret indicates how strongly the 'malign vibes' affect her.

Margaret's alliance with Magnus offers us another dimension to her character. Magnus is mysterious; his madness and his deeply ingrained Scottish culture show him in a world of his own. He claims to have a privileged insight, and there appears to be some truth in this, since he alone knows Margaret and perceives the evil in her; indeed, he admires it for its immoral grandeur. However, Magnus has a wider sense of reality than Margaret. When they discuss her plans for the murder of Hilda, Magnus warns her that, irrespective of her intentions and feelings, 'destiny' is stronger than she.

The notion of destiny is important in this book and appears on many levels. After the murder of Margaret's grandmother, we are told that Margaret's younger sister Jean is sent to a convent school in Liege where she meets a young lover and lives with him happily 'year in, year out'. This sudden and huge perspective gives the book a great sense of inevitable evolution. When Hilda meets Andrew Barnet in the plane on her way to Britain, they both agree that there is no need to fear flying. 'Best to relax, not to think about it,' he says. 'Destiny is destiny.' Hilda rejoins that she too believes in destiny.

Although this encounter is brief, the reader has the impression that both Hilda and Andrew would have been happy to share a destiny different from that which befalls them; the last paragraphs in the book are in the future tense, showing how Andrew will hear of Hilda's death the following day, and how this will suddenly empty his life, and give him a great need to talk of her. Forces beyond human control seemingly eclipse human need, but it is a positive feature of the moral structure of the book that the malevolence of Margaret Murchie has no power against them.

Conclusion

Muriel Spark's women of power are unforgettably formidable. Their strong personalities provide the novels in which they feature with an impressive dynamism. Not only do they fascinate the reader as individuals, but their eccentric and unpredictable behaviour provides an impetus to the development of the narrative.

Miss Brodie's self-indulgent manipulation of her pupils is ironically boosted by their early adolescent predilection for fantasy; they weave their own myths about their teacher with the same credulity as she demands for her own myths. However, it is not her creation of a mythology about herself which triggers the momentum of the narrative, but her plans for the future of those around her, staff and pupils alike. Selina's selfishness, her deliberate selection of Nicholas as someone she can use to her advantage, her total indifference to the suffering of others, eventually prove to be devastatingly illuminating. She changes Nicholas's life.

Alexandra, Abbess of Crewe, is given most licence of all these women. Because her power is created in terms which are themselves obscure and mystifying, the reader simply has no idea what might happen next. She is able to assert her own whim in the way she exercises her power, so that, setting all notions of the power of God aside, she proceeds as if all right over others is her own. Her own fantasies, her own tastes, her own capacity for conspiracy rule supreme.

Maggie is in many ways the victim of her own power. The way in which she uses it is not consciously manipulative nor selfish, but it has effects which eventually put her at risk.

These women of power do not retain their rule. Part of the skill of the construction of the plots in each case ensures that there are, implicitly, other factors at large which have greater force than they. Jean Brodie is deflated by her refusal to admit to any criterion of validity beyond her own perception. The plans she has contrived for her pupils do not succeed; instead these girls develop their own personalities and create their own future. Each finds a relief in ridding herself of her teacher's restrictive influence. Sandy's betrayal of Miss Brodie results from her realization that there are terms beyond those which her teacher has imposed.

Selina Redwood, according to the picture presented of her when Jane tries to contact her former friends of the May of Teck, eventually becomes highly successful at whatever career she has chosen; Jane tells her friend that Selina won't answer the telephone personally, but can only be contacted through 'thousands of secretaries'. One assumes that in terms of her own life, she has not been defeated: there is scope for women like Selina. But in terms of the novel, her lack of compassion is highlighted in a powerful way. Her total indifference to the suffering of others takes away all the glamour of her seductive appearance. Her success in worldly terms is offset by Nicholas's profound commitment and his martyrdom. She is defeated by this spiritual dimension which, paradoxically, her own evil has awakened.

Alexandra's elaborate machinations prove her downfall. It is ironic that no one involved in the plot, except Felicity, is fully aware of her abuse of power. Felicity cannot however be cited as a positive force in the narrative; her advocacy of love and peace are reminiscent of a fashion of the sixties rather than representative of coherent evaluation. However it is apparent to the reader that Alexandra is ultimately defeated by the power she abuses; she is nominally the head of a Christian order but, in defying the axioms of Christianity, she ensures her own downfall. She is a paragon of egocentricity. Maggie is fortunate; she is indebted to her wealth, but it does not corrupt her although it makes her morally lazy and mildly inconsiderate. Her very lack of awareness of her power proves to be her safeguard. However, although in a sense the reader can admire her resilient personality, it must not be overlooked that she declares her need to be evil in order to conserve her wealth. Margaret Murchie combines an eerie link between evil and a nauseatingly pretentious personality: she is as irritating socially as she is unnerving spiritually. Her ultimate defeat, by mere sordid machinations of criminal greed, is a relief. It suggests that someone's malicious fantasies about themselves and others have no fundamental power.

These novels are highly readable and exciting. The reader is sufficiently distanced from these women to view them objectively yet sufficiently enthralled to be as vulnerable as their victims.

— 3 —

WOMEN AS VICTIMS

The characters I have chosen to discuss in this section are all shown to be under severe pressure. In no case is the portrayal of the 'victim' established for the purpose of the consideration of a particular psychology. The victim is often a necessary character, whose problems highlight the web of persecution established by another agent. Once more, Muriel Spark is concerned with personal resources and the degree on which these may be called to confront problems and challenges. We have seen how the 'mature woman' is able to build on the situations which threaten her; a combination of self-respect, a sense of irony and a perceptive insight combine to enable her to create an indomitable state of mind. The women of power with whom we have been concerned are chiefly characterized by their indifference to others, and a relentless determination to impose their own demands. In each case, the personality of the character is the central issue.

The women I shall discuss below are all, except one, overwhelmed by situations not of their own making. The events which befall them and the forces that pursue them disclose more about the nature of evil and malice than about the make-up of the individual minds of the women under threat. None of these women has any remarkable personal qualities; indeed, an element of their vulnerability emerges in a degree of collusion with their victimization, of which they are not always aware.

Dame Lettie Colston: *Memento Mori*

In order to understand the full impact of *Memento Mori*, it is impossible to isolate one experience. All the characters in this book are very old; they all have, in one way or another, to cope with the vicissitudes of age. Lettie Colston is the most unfortunate; her anxieties are the greatest and her death the most appalling. However, an appraisal of her particular case risks being anecdotal, without a full survey of the other characters in the book and some reflection on how they cope with crises.

Most of the characters in this book are ostensibly the victims of an anonymous telephone call. The police are informed, a file is made up. But, as the book develops, we find that these characters are being challenged, not by a subversive criminal, but by their own mortality. The caller, as the more enlightened observe, is Death itself. The words: 'Remember you must die', are the same in each call. But they are spoken in a different voice, in a different way, according to the identity of the receiver of the call. It becomes clear that the impression the caller makes is bound up with the personality of the recipient. Indeed, each is confronted not only with the reminder of his or her ultimate death, but with a fundamental indication of his or her understanding of life. The anonymous telephone call brings their identity into sharp relief, and makes apparent to the reader the scope of the moral resources they have at their disposal.

When the call to Dame Lettie Colston is recounted at the beginning of the book, it is apparent that she has already received similar calls. She knows that the voice will speak before she has time to do so herself. She knows that the message will be the same. As on earlier occasions, the caller rings off as she is asking who he is. She rings the police, as she has been told to, and also her brother Godfrey. Her tone is dismissive: 'There is no danger. It is merely a disturbance,' she tells him. The voice, she says, is 'quite matter-of-fact'. And Lettie too is matter-of-fact; she declares that the man is mad, and is impatient with the police for not having caught him. Lettie, we find, is behaving as she normally does; she is overtly unruffled and competent, refusing to believe that there is any problem that cannot be settled sensibly by the appropriate authorities.

Lettie refuses to question her own judgment in any situation. When she goes to visit Jean Taylor, her sister-in-law's former maid in hospital, she is quite insensitive to the strains and humiliations of living under this regime, where all the old ladies are called 'Granny' and are patronized by the nurses. They are very fortunate, she declares to her brother Godfrey: they have central heating, plenty of company and they all look 'splendid and clean'. She points out to Jean Taylor that in some Balkan countries old parents are thrown out to beg for their keep in winter. Lettie's self-satisfaction makes her quite dismissive of others' misfortunes; when Jean Taylor remarks that being old is like being engaged in a war and witnessing one by one the loss of companions, Lettie decides that her mind is wandering. She has the same response when Jean Taylor suggests she might obey the anonymous telephone call and indeed start to remember she must die. 'Taylor, I do not wish to be advised on how to think,' she comments sharply. Lettie's asperity is due to her basic inability to sympathize with others but in this case it also has roots in a situation which she has now herself forgotten: she and Jean Taylor were once in love with the same man. Jean Taylor finds Lettie's visits invigorating because of this residual enmity. But she too is rapidly forgetting the original reason for it.

The telephone call with its disorientating message is extremely hard for Lettie to come to terms with, although she does her best to make light of it. When the caller rings and her brother is there, she commands him to keep calm and not to shout, but in fact her own body is trembling. She endeavours to follow the dictates of her common sense and tries to identify the 'dangerous lunatic' who is making the calls. She suspects their friend Alec, an aged gerontologist, and writes to him to this effect. She also – somewhat more wildly – suspects the police inspector who is in charge of the investigation about the call.

116

She declares that she consults him so that he does not know that she suspects him.

Her thoughts are becoming increasingly convoluted, although she continues to assert her self-control as best she can. This stressful condition becomes more apparent: when she writes to Godfrey's son Eric whom she also suspects, she notices how shaky her writing is becoming. 'Two thoughts intruded simultaneously. One was: I am really very tired; and the other: I am not a bit tired, I am charging ahead with great energy.'

Despite Lettie's pronouncements about how fit and well she is, her presence of mind is clearly diminishing. When she goes to bed she takes a feather to be a spider and screams. She feels the need for some strength to support her but all the friends of whom she thinks seem to her to be not strong enough. Finally her mind alights on a certain Tempest Sidebottome, a formidable woman acquaintance whose domineering manner, robust health and accumulated energy are of the kind to 'strike despair into the heart of jaded youth'. The idea of Tempest comforts her and she falls asleep with the notion of a great mother figure to sustain her.

However, before long, Tempest Sidebottome is stricken by cancer and dies. In any case, Lettie's anxieties have become increasingly obsessive. She dismisses Jean Taylor's suggestion that she might take a holiday. Instead, to reassure herself, she spends almost an hour every night searching her house for hidden assailants. Her maid Gwen finds her behaviour tiresome and leaves. She tells her boyfriend of her mistress's strange behaviour. The news spreads amongst criminal circles that this old lady is alone amidst her possessions in her house. Intruders break in and batter Lettie to death. As she is being attacked she looks up at her assailant: she is 'amazed by the reality of this'.

Lettie's lack of self-criticism, her bustling arrogance and her mistaken assumptions about the weakness and inadequacy of others prove to be sources of vulnerability. She refuses to listen to Jean Taylor's suggestion that the caller is 'Death himself' who reminds those who have forgotten him of his presence. She refuses in fact to contemplate any idea of her own limitations. Her bloody murder does not result from any metaphysical agency; it is directly the result of her own paranoid searching of her house, which ironically led to rumours of its accessibility. Her surprise at the 'reality' of the attack suggests that she knew subconsciously that she was inventing a scenario of persecution; she had almost developed a pride in being what she called the 'main objective and victim' of her obscure persecutor.

The voice that Dame Lettie hears on the telephone is 'strong and sinister'. In contrast, the voice heard by Charmian Colston, her sister-in-law, is that of 'a civil young man'. Charmian is a vague and gentle old lady, sleepy and forgetful, whose ramblings and occasional confusion are viewed with disdain by her husband Godfrey. He gets irritated with her for imagining at times that the war is still on, or for calling her maid 'Taylor' – the name of her former maid now in hospital. When Charmian answers the telephone to the mystery caller, she is not at all disturbed. She thinks he is a journalist. This is not surprising since the novels which she wrote many years ago have recently enjoyed a revival, and she has been visited by the press. However, Charmian is not a vain person and she responds to the words of her caller with honesty and self-perception:

> Oh, as to that, she said, for the past thirty years and more I have thought of it from time to time. My memory is failing in certain respects. I am gone eighty-six. But somehow I do not forget my death, whenever that will be.

Charmian, for all her muddles, is more astute than the people around her. She has considerable intuition, and retains an essential understanding of the identities of her peers. For this reason both Godfrey, her husband, and Alec Warner, their friend, are afraid of her. Charmian remembers Alec's love affair with her maid, Jean Taylor, a relationship much frowned on in 1907, and which Alec would prefer to forget. Alec's analytical mind, obsessed with the records he is keeping about the effect of old age on his contemporaries, balks at Charmian's 'novelist's mind'. To Charmian, his affair with Jean was 'a dramatic sequence reaching its fingers into all his life's work'. Alec fears that she will embarrass him by referring to this: she is capable, unwittingly, of undermining his chosen identity as a competent, scientific scholar.

Godfrey fears Charmian for other reasons. He has bullied her throughout their marriage, jealous of her achievements and resentful of her charm. His dictatorial restrictions have curbed her enjoyments of her success and of her friendships. However, in the past, Godfrey has been unfaithful to Charmian. His fear is that she will discover this and that his pose as custodian and mentor will be shattered. Ironically, Charmian knows about his infidelities; she also knows that he dreads her knowing and she is sorry for him. However, Mrs Pettigrew, whom Godfrey has recently appointed to help look after Charmian, finds some incriminating papers and proceeds to blackmail Godfrey. Charmian suspects her of this but there is nothing she can do, knowing that to tell Godfrey that his worries are unnecessary will merely demoralize him. Godfrey is the victim of his fears, and Charmian is powerless to help.

Godfrey needs his identity as a strong, sensible man and very much resents ageing. When he finds he has put cakes in his pocket at a tea after a funeral, he is furious and throws them away. His hold on life is strengthened by his sense of Charmian's weakness, on which he insists. Charmian, however, is capable of resisting all attempts to cast her as a senile, confused old lady. When Mrs Pettigrew is appointed, Charmian senses that she poses a threat; she rallies and quite cleverly makes her perceptions clear. When Mrs Pettigrew remarks, patronizingly, 'We are a bit confused again this morning', Charmian retorts wickedly, 'Are you, my dear? What has happened to confuse you?'

She has a great sense of her identity, which gives her a spiritual peace unknown to those around her. This inner tranquillity gives Charmian something which her confusions and lapses of memory cannot erase: she is able to be alone with herself. Nowhere is this more beautifully illustrated than in the episode where, left alone in the house, she decides to make herself a cup of tea. Overwhelmed with trepidation and pleasure, she sets about this task, something quite strange to her now. Despite her frailty, she goes through each step with determination, and after twenty minutes, the tea tray is finally set by the fire, Charmian having brought in all the different parts of the tea set, the pot and the hot water jug, one by one. The performance, during which she is aware of the dangers of scalding herself and of dropping the china, makes her feel strong and fearless. It is an achievement and something she has done for her own sake. Mrs Pettigrew returns and insists cruelly that she, not Charmian, made the tea. But Charmian has proved her independence to herself. Mrs Pettigrew's bullying poses look cheap in comparison.

Charmian decides that she wishes to go into a nursing home: only there will she find privacy and be free from Godfrey's bossy ways and Mrs Pettigrew's intolerable patronizing. Mrs Pettigrew is keen that Charmian should make this decision in order to dispel her influence over Godfrey. But Charmian is not compelled by Mrs Pettigrew's enmity, even when she hints that she might poison her. She senses that this is a melodramatic threat, although it is wearying. Her reservations have more to do with Godfrey than with Mrs Pettigrew. She knows he is vulnerable and that Mrs Pettigrew is exploiting this. He needs her protection. When Godfrey gets the anonymous telephone call, Charmian feels sorry for him 'huddled amongst his bones'. Nevertheless, she makes the decision. Charmian's independence of spirit makes her invulnerable to Mrs Pettigrew's scheming; she is even able to express a genuine admiration for Mrs Pettigrew when she apparently conquers a fit of asthma: 'I envy your courage. I sometimes feel very helpless without my friends around me . . . When my friends were around me every day, what courage I had!'

Jean Taylor is still very fond of her former mistress and knows her well. She realizes how nervous Godfrey is at the prospect of Charmian's discovery of his previous infidelities, but she decides to help matters. She writes down a list of Charmian's infidelities to Godfrey before she entered the Church and when Guy Leet was her lover. This she gives to Alec and implores him to let Godfrey see the list. The effect, as Jean Taylor had anticipated, is to make Godfrey very cheerful and courageous. He and Charmian are able to confront each other without resentment or distress.

The tensions and problems in the relationship between Godfrey and Charmian are resolved, thanks to their eventual ability to face themselves and each other. Charmian's response to the anonymous telephone call is far more composed and untroubled than that of Godfrey. Godfrey, like his sister Lettie, is annoyed and self-righteous; he thinks of writing to *The Times* to express his indignation. Like Lettie, Godfrey has an image of himself which he spends his energy in perpetuating. He is furtive and secretive about his weakness for cakes, and his obsession with catching sight of a lady's revealed ankle. But, above all, he does not wish his past to be known to Charmian and it is this terror of being known which is the source of his torment, and which Mrs Pettigrew is able to exploit. His need to present himself as free from all wrongdoing and all weakness makes him difficult for Charmian to live with; he will not see that she in fact is humouring him, not the other way around. It is only Jean Taylor's wisdom in communicating details of Charmian's infidelities that liberates him from his guilt complex. From that moment on he is prepared to face the truth about himself. At last Charmian has her independence and will be free from the humiliations Godfrey has submitted her to throughout their marriage.

Jean Taylor, Charmian's former maid, does not receive the telephone call; she is in hospital racked with arthritis. Her memento mori is around her; the old ladies in her ward talk of death and some die; the senile patients who are brought into the ward are a constant reminder of debility. Jean Taylor has not needed to be told of the last stage of the human condition; once in the hospital she muses on old age. Her own suffering is acute, both on a physical and on a moral level. The 'lacerating familiarity' of the nurses' attitudes is more painful than the effects of the disease. However, Jean Taylor subdues her experience through her faith and makes of her suffering a devotional offering. In this way she accepts and even celebrates her life in the ward, enjoying the company of her fellow 'grannies' with their cockney exuberance. When Alec Warner offers her the opportunity of going into a nursing home, she refuses. She has given her life meaning where she is. Jean Taylor has lived through the rigours of being 'in service' to a class of which she eventually became part. Her friendship with Charmian, her mistress, and her love affair with Alec made her essentially the social equal of them both. But the disapproval of others suppressed her and she could not find a way to live independently. However, she decided to stay with Charmian whom she dearly loved, despite the restraints of her position. Jean Taylor's wisdom is a point of reference throughout the book. Her comments on the elderly acquaintances around her show that she has no need of the anonymous telephone call. She says to Lettie that it is difficult for old people to remember they must die and that it is best to acquire the habit when young. A brief flashback to her relationship with Alec in 1907 shows that she had already begun to appreciate the importance of a reflection on death. When Alec asks her if she believes in the existence of other people, she replies that the graveyard they can see is a reminder of the existence of other people: 'Why bother to bury people if they don't exist?' Death, ultimately, gives people their identity; it is only in the perspective of their death that they acquire reality. Jean Taylor appreciates the moral value of old age. She declares that even when old people consider themselves restricted and frustrated, they are still fulfilling their lives. She claims that 'a good death', which Alec Warner asks her to look out for in her companions in the ward, resides not in the dignity of bearing but in the disposition of the soul.

Memento Mori is a vindication of integrity. The anonymous telephone call 'concentrates the mind' and the reader can see which of the characters has the integrity to measure up to the reality of the human condition. Dame Lettie will not admit to her vulnerability and anxiety and ultimately finds her worst fears realized – because she has not wished to acknowledge them. Alec Warner has diverted himself from the reality of his own condition by obsessively compiling observations on that of others; he has insisted on a clinical, scientific version of life. This approach makes it impossible for him to have close relationships with others – his manner is patronizing and distant. When his records are destroyed in a fire, he feels that he too has died. Only Charmian with her intuition and deep charity, and Jean Taylor with her hard-earned wisdom show themselves to have fulfilled the blessing of life. They do not look for solutions in bureaucracy but rely on their faith and inner warmth for enlightenment.

Lettie Colston is a victim of her own pretentiousness. It would be wrong to see this deficiency as the most significant feature of the momentum of the narrative. The focus of the novel is broader than this one particular case; all the characters are seen coping with the various defects their personalities have developed in the course of their lives. As we have seen, Jean Taylor and Charmian have the sensitivity and patience to accept the implications of their old age and to retain the essential features of their personalities, unassailed by the animosity and resentfulness of others. Perhaps the most important function of the character of Lettie Colston in the novel is to demonstrate how much she lacks these qualities. The degree to which Lettie is affected by the telephone call reveals her vulnerability which her bustling officiousness has only served to disguise. In her claims to superiority over everyone else and her dismissive rejections of others' difficulties, she has dehumanized herself. The telephone call is a reminder of her humanity, which she has no resources to counter.

Alice Dawes: *The Bachelors*

Alice Dawes is an unconscious victim in this book. She is unaware of the malevolence which has penetrated her life.

Her mind is simple and impressionable. Her lover, Patrick Seton, is the focal point of her life; she defends him furiously, convinced that he is sensitive and gifted. She has no idea that he is plotting her death. In creating Alice Dawes, Muriel Spark shows that she is capable of compassion in her narrative presentation. She does not mock her simplicity. However, she is not indulgent either. Alice's vow not to believe in God if Patrick is convicted of blackmail, is heavily ironic. Alice does not question her own interpretations; she has convinced herself that Patrick loves her and that he is a good man. She has no concept of God, except as a kind of insurance policy for things turning out right. The reader learns much from the diametrically opposed perspectives of Alice's understanding and the truth.

The Bachelors is a book about the insidious workings of spiritualism. Patrick Seton (a name not far removed from Satan) is a successful medium, and a coterie of admiring fellow spiritualists has grown up around him. Their belief in Patrick's powers gives him an aura on which he thrives, and which puts his devotees at considerable risk. At the opening of the book we learn that a court case is shortly to take place in which a follower of Patrick Seton, a certain Freda Flower, is to accuse him of swindling her out of her savings. He has produced a letter which he claims was written by Freda Flower, in which she states her desire to give him her money to advance his ministry. She denies having written this letter.

The book is not merely concerned with plots to deceive and manipulate. What emerges most forcefully is Patrick Seton's power. His impact on those susceptible to him is so devastating that even Freda Flower, who knows that Patrick has forged the damaging letter, is in two minds about whether to go ahead with the case. He has taken away her confidence and she is no longer clear about the truth: 'he can look you in the eyes', she says, 'and tell a lie so that you would believe that you were telling the lie not him.' Overtly a repressed man who talks in a barely audible voice which trails away at the end of his sentences, Patrick's performance as a medium is overwhelming.

Patrick had gone under in style with a quivering of the lower lip and chin, upturned eyes and convulsive whinnies. A few threads of ectoplasm, like white tape in the dim light, proceeded from the corners of his mouth. Then, in a voice hugely louder than his own, he announced, 'I am now coming in touch with the control ...'

Certainly the members of the 'Wider Infinity' are totally convinced by Patrick's powers and await with excitement and dread what message he might pass on to them. The narrator's description of Patrick whilst he is in a trance suggests that he is genuinely unconscious and that he has undergone a radical physical change whilst 'giving utterance'. However, the message which he transmits to Freda Flower just before the beginning of her court case against him is one which it is in his interest to convey: he tells her that her dead husband is instructing 'the sister with a name like a plant' not to 'act against another of the brethren'. If she does, she will be in peril, he adds. Considering how the skin of Patrick's face is clinging to his bones, that his mouth had widened about two inches and that his voice is clanging out to betoken the presence of his spirit guide, it is not surprising that Freda Flower is distressed and feels reluctant to continue her case against him.

Patrick's followers, of the 'Wider Infinity' and its select power group the 'Inner Spiral', are mostly middle-aged women, together with some bachelors. However, there are bachelors in the book who are not spiritualists but who relate in some way to the coterie. One of these is Ronald Bridges. He is a handwriting expert and has been called to give evidence in the court case about the letter purported to have been written by Freda Flower. This is, initially, the only link he has with Patrick whom he sees for the first time at the beginning of the book. Ronald's importance in the book is greater than this incidental role would suggest. He is an epileptic and the rigours he must endure as a consequence of his illness have led to the formation of a strong moral sense.

Ronald's Catholicism, his acceptance of the afflictions of his epilepsy, his grim self-knowledge which leads him to exercises of self-rebuke and penitence, create a polarity: the antithesis of Patrick Seton. Ironically, the manifestations of Ronald's epileptic fits resemble Patrick's condition when in his medium's trance. Patrick, indeed, fetches drugs from his doctor which induce symptoms of epilepsy. Ronald's faith has taught him how to cope with his disease; he prepares himself for an unexpected fit, he carries pills to take as he feels himself succumb, he keeps beside him a wedge of cork to put into his mouth as the first signs seize him. He even cultivates a method to keep conscious as long as possible during a fit. His relationship with his illness has developed from a conversation he once had with an old priest with whom he was discussing his sense of vocation. The priest pointed out that he had no vocation; the affliction of epilepsy, which had been imposed on him, showed that. The priest said that Ronald was never meant to be a first-rate careerist. When Ronald reasoned ironically, 'Only a first-rate epileptic?', the priest told him that this was so.

It is clear that Ronald's struggle to lead as positive a life as possible and to accept his suffering with dignity does, indeed, suggest a kind of spiritual pilgrimage. His faith is his identity. He says that being a Catholic is part of his human existence. Because of his strong identification with his faith, he draws on it to help him establish an understanding of other people. When the letter he has to examine publicly in the law case against Patrick Seton is stolen from his office, he is laid low with a deep melancholy. He recites a passage from the letter to the Philippians to protect his mind. Slowly he is able to 'wrench his mind' into a positive appreciation of the qualities of the people around him, the thought of whom had been filling him with nausea. When later he suffers a fit, he goes to confession so that through receiving absolution, he receives a 'sign of friendly recognition' from God. Ronald is perceived by his friends as wise; he is often consulted, he says, on the advisability of marriage. Matthew, a journalist friend, comes to discuss his own case with Ronald and they both agree that the Catholic faith advises strongly that a man should choose between the priesthood or wedlock. Ronald is reluctant to marry, although he has had a close relationship with an attractive Swedish girl, Hildegarde. His way of life is essentially solitary and his earlier conviction that he had a vocation for the priesthood is reflected in his response to others. He disciplines his mind to think generously of people.

His faith is more than a discipline; he has a strong intuition, bordering on the prophetic. He states that he believes in telepathy; he also declares that it is surely possible to contact the spirits of the dead. This mystic element of his mind is linked to an insight which gives him almost supernatural foreknowledge of the outcome of events. He says, for example, that Patrick Seton will be convicted. He states that Patrick was never married, although he claims to be. All these aspects of Ronald's sensibility demonstrate how close he is in fact to the powers which Patrick Seton so spectacularly and so horrifically exploits. The stress and helplessness which Ronald's epilepsy brings into his life are deliberately cultivated by Patrick when he takes drugs to help him to go into a trance. Whereas Ronald has a basic respect for the dignity of others and a sense of his own fallibility, Patrick Seton considers himself beyond the demands of responsible behaviour; it is part of his character to wield power and manipulate. Ronald says that there are only two types of religion: the spiritualist and the Catholic. The implication of this statement is that the forces which act in the metaphysical dimension are recognized in both faiths. In spiritualism, however, the mysteries of prophetic insight and of the afterlife are exploited and played with; their manifestation is essentially ambiguous. Only Catholicism offers a structure to contain understanding of these forces and through Christ, to explain their relevance to the life of men.

The contrast and links between Ronald and Patrick are essential to an understanding of the way in which Muriel Spark considers the mysteries and ironies of faith. However, *The Bachelors* is a novel, not a contemplative piece of prose and it is in terms of their action that we see most clearly defined the characters of Ronald and Patrick. In order to bring out fully the inherent evil of Patrick's sinister machinations, the narrative focuses on his relationship with Alice Dawes. Alice is a young, attractive but simple-minded girl who works in an espresso coffee bar. She is in love with Patrick Seton and expecting his baby. Patrick has told Alice that he will marry her, but first has to wait for his divorce to come through. Alice trusts him implicitly. Her friend Elsie finds it difficult to understand Alice's infatuation with Patrick; to Elsie he is eerie and not at all seductive. But Alice defends her lover against her friend's criticism: 'He's *got* something,' she declares. When they are alone together he is wonderful, she says: he recites poetry, he is a 'sort of real artist'. Above all Alice claims 'he's got a soul'. The reader soon learns that Alice is in an extremely vulnerable position. She is pregnant, tired and still working, but her main physical affliction is that she is diabetic. She is completely within Seton's power as Elsie observes to Matthew. Only on one point does she resist him: he wants her to have an abortion. She refuses.

As the book moves on it becomes apparent that Seton has made up his own mind how to deal with this situation. He has devised a plot whereby he can cause Alice's death. Seton once received whilst in a trance indications that a certain doctor had been involved in some scandalous dealings. Seton, whilst not fully aware of the facts of the affair which his medium's powers have touched on, is nonetheless happy to exploit his hold over the doctor. He goes to him for money and for drugs which bring on symptoms of epilepsy. Now he turns to him for information about how to bring about Alice's death through deprivation of insulin. He asks the doctor if he may borrow his chalet in Switzerland to take Alice on holiday. Dr Lyte slowly realizes Patrick's intentions but feels utterly powerless to intervene. His plot to kill Alice obsesses Seton to the point where, even when standing in the dock at the time of his trial for fraudulence, he imagines her lying on the mountainside, crumpled up with an overdose of insulin.

Alice is totally trusting of Seton and this blind trust makes his plot even more insidious. The reader is told that from his early youth Seton had become a thief, cajoling people who trusted him. He sees himself as above the moral claims to which others submit. Ronald remarks that were Patrick to consider his private life honestly, he would feel as nauseated as he, Ronald, did before a fit. But Patrick regards himself as exempt from any responsibility. He tells himself that, through murdering Alice, he will 'liberate her spirit'. Sex he sees as basically disgusting; the baby Alice has conceived disgusts him equally.

The foul way in which Seton's mind works links with his alarming appearance when in a trance; the diabolic connotations are clear. At one point, when he has 'gone under' the only sinister words he utters are: 'I creep'.

Alice's inability to sense her lover's true character makes her strangely innocent. Every day she goes to church, praying that Seton should not be convicted. She calls her prayers 'a test of God'. 'If Patrick doesn't get off I don't believe in God,' she says. Ronald, with his intuitive capacity, has sensed that Patrick Seton is a danger to Alice. He tells her never to expect anything of him and to leave him. But, coming out of the blue, this means nothing to Alice. She is ironically committed to her lover, unaware that she stands between the forces of darkness and of light.

Seton is convicted and eventually we are told that Alice marries Matthew, the inebriated Irish journalist who long ago conceived a passion for her, and, with Ronald's encouragement, waited patiently until she was free from her obsession. We are told little about her feelings at this point but it would appear that she adjusted to the situation even though her first reaction to Seton's conviction was to declare that she no longer believed in God.

The Bachelors is conceived in several dimensions. The reader must follow through the imaginative exercise of experiencing the events and confrontations of the narrative from different points of view. Muriel Spark describes spiritualism without ridicule; her account of Patrick's performance as a medium borders on the supernatural; it is clear that he is able to ascertain elements of the lives of people around him without full consciousness of what he is relating. The extreme physical change and mental exhaustion he is seen to experience suggest a genuine ability to pass from one state of consciousness into another. Although Spark is witty about the attitudes of some of Seton's devotees, the implication of the narrative is that spiritualism is a frightening form of self-indulgence at the expense of true understanding of sacred mysteries. The way in which this dimension of the narrative is presented involves the reader in the full impact of this sinister practice. Ronald's epilepsy is another level of experience in which the reader is involved. The threats, discomfort and debility brought into Ronald's life by his epilepsy render his self-discipline and sensitivity more admirable; we witness these qualities as weapons of self-defence in a personal struggle and thus they lose any overtones of dogmatism or moralizing. Thus, two characters above all, Seton and Ronald Bridges, draw the reader into a wide range of experience and present fundamental questions.

Alice, on the other hand, is presented far more superficially. She is the victim of Seton's manoeuvres and of his sinister mentality but her lack of awareness of this removes her from the reader's immediate identification or close sympathy. Her innocence and vulnerability, however, highlight the moral opposition which Ronald and Patrick Seton play out and make its implications more accessible to the reader.

Annabel Christopher: *The Public Image*

Several of Muriel Spark's books are deliberately set in a specific social climate and this climate has an important function in the narrative. *The Public Image* is one of these. However, we never find Spark identifying the origins of the predicament of her characters in social terms. These lie basically in far more profound areas: the relationship of the characters with themselves, with those close to them. Annabel Christopher is ostensibly the victim of the film world in which she works; but a close reading of this book shows that the forces which undermine her are jealousy and deceit. Her own ignorance of the existence of these forces makes her vulnerable to them.

Unlike other women in Muriel Spark's novels, Annabel Christopher is insipid. However, she is photogenic and this quality leads to a successful career in films. Her director fabricates for her a public image, an essential element, it appears, to ensure the impact made by a film actress. Annabel eventually becomes a victim, not of her public image, but of the effect it has on her husband. This novel has a moral theme which is not spelt out in any way; however, it emerges that a travesty of the truth has damaging consequences. The identities of the main characters, Annabel and her husband Frederick, become unstable to the point where they know neither themselves nor each other. The choice Annabel is forced to make at the end of the book is a choice between truth and falsehood, between a life which leaves her free and a world of fabrication which seeks only to exploit.

The book opens at a point which ultimately is shown to be pivotal in the narrative: Annabel has just installed herself in a flat in Rome which she has acquired entirely through her own efforts. She is there alone with her baby when Billy, an old friend of Annabel's and of her husband, bursts in and demands if her new flat is intended to promote her public image. This question leads on to an extensive flashback in the narrative which recounts the circumstances of Annabel's career and the development of her public image.

It is emphasized that Annabel was stupid and the narrator alludes to her stupidity with a tone of disdain. We are told that Annabel was ignorant of her stupidity, also that she had no strength of personality nor even charm of physical presence. However, merely by 'playing herself in a series of poses' as she was directed, Annabel was able to project what was demanded of her; the camera transformed her insignificant looks into an impression of beauty. Annabel was not a passionate person. She

131

had married a fellow drama student when very young and worked in various jobs as well as playing the few small roles that came her way. She was not ambitious whereas Frederick, her husband, had a deep conviction that his talents were such as to suit him for major parts only, which unfortunately he was never offered. Frederick brooded much over the lack of opportunity to fulfil his potential whereas Annabel was content with whatever turned up, feeling deeply about nothing. Even the two afternoons she spent in bed with Billy, their friend and fellow student, roused her little; she felt nothing for him and no guilt nor self-reproach either at having betrayed her husband. Slowly however, Annabel becomes mildly interested in the progress of her career. She does not identify in the slightest with the image her director has dreamt up for her – a sultry, highly-sexed woman beneath a veneer of self-control and good breeding – but she is fascinated by its success and by her ability to play it apparently just by existing. She is pleased by what the narrator calls tartly 'her meagre skill and her many opportunities to exercise it'. Apart from being intrigued by the ease with which she is able to do well in the film business, Annabel is not particularly affected by any other aspect of it. She is indifferent to the large sums of money she makes. She is unperturbed by bad reviews of her films; indeed, if some appear, they make her laugh. The only indication of any sense of commitment to her profession she might have is an account of how she avoided a row with her husband which was distracting her by remembering that she had to rise early the following morning and that after a row she would not look good on camera. Despite her success, she remains quite unsophisticated. One friendship, however, has taught her the art of making catty remarks; this is with the wealthy socialite, Golly Mackintosh. Annabel does not change basically, despite this new mannerism. Only one event alters her life totally and that is the birth of her baby. She cares passionately for him and does not wish him to become in any way a part of her career. She refuses to let him be photographed. While she is working she rings his nurse every three hours to find out how he is. Although Luigi, her director, insists that Annabel has become what he has made her, the baby brings a reality into her life which is quite independent of her success in films, of Luigi's efforts to form her personality and of her marriage. The beginning of *The Public Image*, set in the flat which she has organized and where she is briefly but blissfully alone with her baby, emphasizes her achievement in at last defining her identity. This is made clear from the positive description given of Annabel's affection for the view from her flat of the 'narrow streets intertwined with narrow lines, the twisty minds of history'. The narrator now identifies with Annabel, whereas previously she had been viewed with a distinct lack of warmth, one might almost say with contempt.

Annabel's success in the film world is not half as significant as her achievement in surviving the hostility of her husband. By finding the flat in Rome and installing herself in it with her baby, she has for the first time asserted herself independently both of her director and of her husband. She has been aware of his restlessness, conscious of his unfaithfulness to her. She has borne his taunts and insults with little resistance. Her somewhat phlegmatic nature rather than strength of character has made this possible and so her lack of resentment towards Frederick's unpleasantness is not presented as a particularly endearing trait. However, her love for her baby has given her a positive rather than a negative personality. It is ironic that just at this point in the narrative Frederick's jealousy and vindictiveness are about to surface in a quite unpredictable and horrific way.

Frederick, we are told, is an 'untrained intellectual'. As Annabel's career takes off, he becomes increasingly moody and often angry. It is clear that he derives no pleasure from her success but resents it. He is a man obsessed with his own merits, and Annabel's good fortune in her director and in being photogenic infuriate Frederick. He finds it quite unfair that with so little talent she should be regarded as so gifted. A fundamental source of resentment to Frederick is Annabel's approach to acting. Frederick had shone at drama school; he considers himself to be a brilliant actor. His theories about acting demand total identification with the role on the part of the actor; he should endorse the character's emotional response with his own. To Frederick Annabel is superficial. She has no such deep feelings; to her acting is merely a form of deception.

Their relationship deteriorates under these pressures. To Annabel, Frederick's moods and furies are merely irritating. She does her best not to let them upset her. She does not reproach him for living off her earnings and her only fear is that he might interfere with her career by throwing his weight around the studio. However, Frederick's feelings are far deeper and more complex than these. He has used Annabel's passivity and her lack of ambition to promote his own self-importance. Her character has not changed basically but the response of the world has, and this is what he resents. He is no longer content with his own life and even though he has the opportunity to write film scripts, is given his own public image as an introverted intellectual Englishman who adores his wife, is able to have affairs without incurring Annabel's complaints, he still feels trapped and in some obscure way exploited. Annabel, although she has no intellectual power of perception, has a degree of intuitive wisdom; she is aware that Frederick has a 'private self-image of seriousness' and that she is a threat to this. Annabel is not crushed by her public image of the 'tiger lady'; she finds it amusing and harmless. But Frederick is deeply oppressed by the way in which he is seen as a mere appendage to Annabel.

Finally he wreaks his revenge. He kills himself and has carefully devised the scenario in such a way that Annabel's public image will be destroyed. He leaves several suicide notes in which he claims that Annabel's wild life and infidelity have driven him to despair. He sends members of Rome's bohemian fringe to Annabel's flat early in the evening, telling them they are invited to a party; many of these people are drugged or drunk. When Annabel is called to identify his body, she feels quite numb, 'overwhelmed by his unspeakable trick'. Billy comes to her and tells her that he has all Frederick's suicide notes in his possession. Annabel quickly realizes that she must do her utmost to protect her image and to resist the scandal which Frederick's 'unspeakable trick' would lead to, if his ruse were successful.

At this point the degree to which Annabel's public image has become important to her becomes apparent. She appears to feel no distress about Frederick's suicide; indeed, she puts it to the back of her mind so successfully that she goes to sleep thinking she must remind Frederick not to mention the party. She is fully conscious, however, of how cleverly Frederick has set up this plot against her and she fears profoundly that his assessment is right: if her public image is destroyed, she will have no future. She sets about trying to shore up the damage. She insists on talking to the press although her doctors advise against it, and surrounds herself with her neighbours who create a frame of compassion for her apparent grief. She states publicly that she refuses to believe that Frederick killed himself. Later she suggests that Frederick was in fact pursued to his death by amorous women. To begin with it seems that her challenge to Frederick's machinations has worked. Her experience has enabled her to recognize the 'professional nature of the enemy' and she has hit back with her own professional skill. During the whole of this episode Annabel is in control of herself, the demands of her 'image' directing her to present a specific version of affairs to which all else is subservient. Even her baby, who hitherto she has kept away from the photographers, is held close to her 'like a triumphant shield'. Her director Luigi is surprised at her tenacity; he points out that her image can be changed: she can become known as a 'wild woman' and play different roles. But Annabel is adamant: 'It's the widowed tiger lady or nothing,' she states.

Annabel has in fact felt protected by her image. The demure veneer ascribed to her matched well with her impassive character; the fiction was the implication that an intense sexuality lay behind this appearance. All Annabel had to do was merely to hide what was not there. However, although her care in sustaining the image after Frederick's death is thus far successful, she is conscious, in a way that had never before struck her, of the savage disparity between truth and fiction. The doctor's daughter, Gelda, brings home the truth with a clarity that embarrasses and alarms Annabel: 'Why did he commit suicide and make a scandal for you?' she enquires. Annabel wants the child to go; she could demolish the fiction on which Annabel was now utterly dependent.

All Annabel's efforts were to be in vain. Billy has photocopied the suicide notes and is preparing to blackmail Annabel with them through her lawyer, Tom. Tom advises paying Billy. But suddenly Annabel changes. She wants to be as free as her baby, she decides. And taking her baby she leaves the court unnoticed, having presented Frederick's letters to the judge. She catches a plane anonymously. She has turned her back on her career.

Annabel's action is no moral triumph; she is not shown to have any deep reflective powers, nor any tendency to make assessments of those around her. However, with the birth of her child, she is governed by an instinct which at last gives her an authenticity. When she is briefly alone with her child she realizes what she values. She has an interior life now which she is anxious to protect: she has a sense of reality which contrasts with the sophisticated manoeuvring of the cinema world. The narrator tells us that 'she feared to display her emotions in case they melted away like some public image'. When Frederick tells Annabel condescendingly that she is like an empty shell, we can see that in a way he is right. But with her baby, her existence has a meaning, a purpose, and it is a deep organic purpose, the significance of which lies far beyond the trivialities of the fallacious film world. She has a fundamental identity which she derives from being human and having a child, 'as an empty shell contains by its very structure the echo and harking image of former and former seas'.

In opting out of the film world, Annabel is following through a decision she has already made intuitively. She has, since his birth, been determined to keep her child away from the world in which she works. She is instinctively aware that it threatens and destroys. When she is endeavouring to reconstruct her public image after Frederick's devastating attempt to ruin it, she finds herself running round in circles, working harder and harder to conceal the truth. It is a vicious circle. To collude with the demands of this ethos is to assume its decadence. Eventually she realizes that for her own sake as well as for that of her child, she must break away.

Although Spark's narrative is somewhat scathing towards Annabel in the earlier part of the book, she presents her later on in an increasingly compassionate light. Her sympathy, however, does not lie with Annabel's initially successful attempts to forestall Frederick's plan; Annabel attains true dignity when she admits defeat and no longer wants to win.

Lise: *The Driver's Seat*

Nowhere in Muriel Spark's work is a character presented so remotely as Lise in *The Driver's Seat*. Her behaviour is never explained, merely described. She has no clear intentions as far as the reader can make out. Her feelings are never intimated; the reader can only make wild guesses at them, whilst trying to make sense of her erratic speeches and actions. Her very inaccessibility is a disturbing yet compulsive feature of the narrative. The style of the account is as bizarre as Lise herself; it is in the present tense, which emphasizes the narrator's detachment as each moment is carefully picked out without comment. However, occasionally the tense leaps forward into the future, indicating a further alarming and inevitable dimension. From the statements about what will happen the following day, it becomes clear that Lise will be murdered. And it also becomes clear that she herself has all the time been wholly complicit in this event.

Ostensibly, then, this is a new kind of thriller with a highly obscure plot, intended to mystify and shock. However, it is possible to identify in Lise's portrayal elements which link her character with her death. Everything she says and does is a denial of life, not in the sense that she is withdrawn or depressive as a suicidal person might be, but in her total defiance and rejection of other people. Her deliberate antipathy and deceit towards those she meets suggest that any ability to respond or identify with others is quite dead in her. The negative features of her character are equally as horrifying as her death; and ultimately indicate the cause of her complicity in her murder.

At the outset of the narrative Lise is described as an office worker, very hard-working and intractably efficient. Her apartment is similarly Spartan; it is a pinewood interior, everything designed to fold neatly away. Lise keeps it 'as clean-lined and clear . . . as if it were uninhabited'. Spark writes of the apartment: 'The swaying tall pines among the litter of cones on the forest floor have been subdued into silence and into obedient bulks.' Lise's life would appear to be equally subdued; it is totally disciplined and colourless. What little description we have of her personal appearance suggests a similar absence of vitality:

> Her lips, when she does not speak or eat, are normally pressed together like the ruled line of a balance sheet marked straight with her old-fashioned lipstick, a final and judging mouth . . .

Lise's action at the beginning of the novel in buying a highly-coloured dress is clearly at odds with the account of her usual appearance. Her fury with the shop assistant who tells her that the material of the dress she first tries on is stain-resistant, marks yet another departure from her habitual constraint. We are told that she is about to take a holiday. But there is nothing relaxed or festive about Lise's purchase; indeed, it is already sinister. Her insistence on having a material that holds stains is odd. Having rejected the dress and loudly proclaimed her distaste, she flounces out of the shop. She is, however, satisfied 'at her own dominance over the situation'. Clearly, the image of Lise as a woman wanting power is sustained here, despite the anomaly of her strange desire for a highly-coloured dress from which stains cannot be removed. But it is again obvious that she is behaving uncharacteristically in, for some reason, seeking attention. When she passes through the airport the following day, we are told that people will remember having seen her. She also makes herself noticeable by adopting a very high-pitched voice when she speaks. Her intentions, her motives are quite opaque.

There is no indication that she is mad. There is, implicitly, some kind of rationale in her mind and a determination to follow it through. This is for the first time apparent when she pursues, quite deliberately, a fellow passenger who has, for some reason, made an important impression on her. She sits down in the plane next to him and quite suddenly he reacts to her presence with great fear. He leaves his seat hastily to sit elsewhere. Later Lise will befriend this man's aunt in the hotel where she is staying. Later still he will arrive at the hotel himself and Lise will persuade him to murder her.

It is not until these events are recounted that the trend to Lise's actions makes some sense. Her close examination of a paperknife at the airport gift shop links up with her accompanying Mrs Fiedke, a fellow guest at her hotel, to purchase a similar knife in a department store in the town where they are staying; this is a gift for Mrs Fiedke's nephew and it is with this knife that he will cut Lise's throat. The connection between Lise's sighting of the dark-suited man in the airport lounge and subsequent events is revealed only by the outcome of these events. Even then it is not clear to the reader how Lise could have been able to identify this man as a psychopath who had a history of attacking women, nor how she could have discerned a link between him and Mrs Fiedke at the hotel. The implication is that Lise had some strange intuition, similar in fact to her murderer's unaccountable recognition of her on the plane and his resulting fear.

There is, then, no underlying chain of events and circumstances which lend an alternative meaning to the narrative. The occasional confusion of Lise herself suggests her own lack of full understanding of what is happening. She is driven by some inner compulsion, but does not appear to have a clear directive. She is looking for a particular person, she identifies him, but still appears to be looking. After the dark-suited man changes his seat in the plane, she appears to give up her pursuit of him. Meantime, she continues to respond in a strange fashion to other men she meets. She is approached on the plane by Bill, who is determined to befriend her in a flirtatious way. Bill is highly egocentric, he is deeply involved in campaigning for macrobiotic food and calls himself an 'enlightenment leader'. He continually tells Lise that he is 'her type' and, although she is initially unimpressed, she condescends eventually to be friendly towards him. He is adamant in his attachment to her, and sufficiently obsessed by his own dogmatic statements about diet not to be puzzled or put off by her behaviour. But all the time it is clear that Lise has her mind on someone or something else and is not keen to deepen her relationship with Bill. After the aircraft lands she becomes interested in a pallid, sickly-looking man, apparently related to the aristocracy. But he is collected by staff and Lise is once more despondent. Indeed she starts to cry, saying that she is sure 'he was the one' she had to meet. Bill consoles her and she lets him kiss her. Her preference for the other two men she has encountered appears doubly uncanny when it becomes clear that she has been looking not for a lover but for a murderer.

Her subsequent behaviour on her brief holiday is apparently motiveless. She upbraids the maid at the hotel for leaving a toothglass in her room with an unused Alka Seltzer in it. She unpacks her bag with utmost care. She scrutinizes closely a map of the town where she is staying. The narrator offers no enlightenment; indeed, questions are provoked in the reader's mind. The narrator queries: 'Who knows her thoughts? Who can tell?' Her appearance, as she leaves the hotel to go into the town, is shocking. Not only do the raucous colours of her dress and mackintosh stand out, but also the hem of her dress is unfashionably long (the book is set in the style of the sixties) and, the narrator tells us, she looks, beside the mini-skirted girls of the town, like a street prostitute. Her loud appearance and odd behaviour are briefly attenuated by her befriending of

Mrs Fiedke with whom she agrees to share a taxi. When the old lady thanks her, Lise says, unusually: 'One should always be kind in case it might be the last chance.' In retrospect, it is obvious that Lise knows she will not have many chances to be kind henceforth. Also, since it is Mrs Fiedke's nephew whom she will eventually persuade to kill her, it will also be clear that her intentions are not fundamentally kind at all. Indeed, within a short time of staying in her company, she terrifies Mrs Fiedke with her loud, harsh laughter. Lise behaves in a senseless and flirtatious manner to two men she meets subsequently, a TV salesman in a department store and a garage man whom she encounters when sheltering from a student demonstration in the street. She puts on an amazing performance for this man, claiming to be an intellectual widow who teaches in New Jersey. He finds her attractive and has the impression she is inviting him to make love to her. Eventually she manages to elude his embraces and steals his car.

Towards the end of the book Lise is in the Hilton Hotel, apparently still in pursuit of the person she claims to be trying to find. There she sees the sickly-looking man whom she noticed on the plane. But then she decides he is 'not her type' after all. She meets up with Bill, the macrobiotic, once more and persuades him to drive her to a park which she has identified on her map. She examines the pavilion in the park with meticulous attention; Bill laughs and says she is behaving like a gangster planning a hold-up. In this short sequence with Bill, Lise does appear to feel some deep emotion, although her character has hitherto been presented with so little indication of her feelings that it is hard to tell when she is not simply play-acting. At this point, however, she tells Bill he knows nothing about her and says that she feels lonely. She repudiates Bill's advances, implying that she has no interest in or desire for sex. Since Bill professes to be merely concerned that he should keep up with his regime of a daily orgasm, his warmth towards her is hardly likely to change her attitude. While Bill witters on about Yin and Yang, she says to him that she wants to go home 'and feel all that lonely grief again'. Although this is quite a moving statement, it is hard to relate to anything we have known of Lise before and, once again, it is unclear if she is saying anything meaningful at all. Bill pulls her down on to the concrete but she escapes and drives off, having alerted passers-by with her screams. Bill is taken into custody, thus providing him with an excellent alibi when Lise is found stabbed to death the following morning.

Lise returns to the hotel and there finds Mrs Fiedke's nephew, the man she was drawn to on the plane. She has no hesitation in ordering him to accompany her and drives off with him to the park. He is afraid. He admits he has attacked women before but claims now to be cured and to wish for a normal life. But Lise soon succeeds in compelling him to set about her murder. She tells him where and how to strike, giving him for the purpose the paper-knife his aunt bought for him. As he cuts her throat she screams, 'evidently perceiving how final is finality'. He performs the murder precisely to her instructions. He is subsequently arrested and tells the police the unlikely tale of Lise's instructions to kill her. The book ends with a description of the sounds made by the barking policemen, the flashing of their epaulettes and the other trappings 'devised to protect them from the indecent exposure of fear and pity'.

Lise is, without doubt, a victim of herself. Her personality is presented blandly. She has no attractive or interesting qualities, other than her inscrutability. The contact she makes with others is inauthentic and unappealing; we cannot identify with her at all. Even her death does not make much impact; we have been alerted to it several times in the narrative and so little are we drawn to her, that we care for her life no more greatly than she does herself. In no other of Muriel Spark's books are both narrator and reader so far outside the central character. By contrast the style and content of *The Driver's Seat* demonstrate how involving are the plots and characters of Spark's other works. However, there is a moral texture, albeit negative, to this piece of writing. We are repulsed by a character for whom life has no meaning; who is entirely without a sense of values within, and without any ability or desire to involve herself with others except to procure a means for her death.

Conclusion

The characters discussed above are all victims in very different situations. However, they are all, and Lise exceptionally, complicit in their victimization.

Lettie Colston considers herself to be very well organized; she has a category for every situation and is expert at deciding on an appropriate response to any problem. Because she has such confidence in her own abilities, she is contemptuous of others who seem less adept. It is her refusal to see anything more complex in life than an administrative problem that leads her to helpless confusion when she receives the telephone call. Her initial resolution of the problem is to inform the police, then she suspects the police, then she suspects her acquaintances. Basically she is suspicious of all other people, hence her insensitivity and her lack of compassion. She ultimately becomes obsessive about checking for the presence of strangers in her house. Ironically this obsession leads to the publicizing of her well-monied solitude and she is indeed attacked. This is a chain of events but it is not without psychological explanation. Lettie's fundamental mistrust of people lays her open to victimization; she is likely to take exception to anyone.

Alice Dawes in *The Bachelors* is vulnerable because of her simple-mindedness. Although it is true to say that she is too gullible and should have had her suspicions about Patrick Seton, she is a likeable person. Her adoration of Patrick is misplaced, but has the credibility of all infatuation. Because of this, Seton's sinister plotting emerges as all the more vile. Eventually Alice avoids being the victim of Seton's plot, but through no resources of her own. In Christian terms she has been given grace, at the very moment when she swears she no longer believes in God. She is an innocent victim but innocence is not a strong quality in this situation; it means more that she is stupid and unperceiving. Her lack of malevolence and her staunch if misplaced loyalty would appear to make her worthy of grace.

Annabel Christopher does have resources to combat the jealousy and exploitation which undermine her. However, these are intuitive and do not emerge from an inner conscious wrestling with her problems. For much of the time she is complicit with the forces round her; she is happy to comply with the demands of her image for the sake of her career, even though she is aware of the falsity of the whole enterprise. It is only when she finds herself on the point of being swallowed up by the whole process of fabrication that she makes the intuitive decision to break free of the world of exploitation.

Lise's horrific plot for her own immolation is the most nauseating of Spark's narratives. We may safely assume that our sense of nausea is deliberately induced; at no point is there any attempt to present Lise in a light that would draw on the reader's sympathy or compassion. Her deception, her remoteness, her coldness, her unpredictability, all serve to alienate her from our capacity for identification. The style of the narrative is clipped and objective. Its pace is calculated and does not seek to involve the reader in the pace of events themselves which are consequently lifeless and unreal. Lise's negative character throws into clear relief the passion and the drive of the many women Spark has created who determine to identify and ally themselves with the positive forces in life. It is clear that such a chance is not an element of personality but a conscious choice. Lise's morbidity demonstrates the horror of the negative use of free will.

NARRATIVE AND FAITH

Muriel Spark's concept of faith is an essential feature of her work. It supplies perspective and balance. Without an appreciation of it, her novels may only be valued for their wit, their irony, their unpredictability. These are indeed attractive aspects of her writing. However, they do not function merely to tease, surprise and entertain. They exist to illustrate a life which is essentially fragmented.

In a world where nothing can be fully grasped, there are dangers; the most threatening is a misplaced confidence in a single selfish viewpoint. Such an error constitutes an essential sin in Christian terms: it is *philautia*, love of self. St Augustine described sin as a turning away from God towards the self. Sin in Christian terms is negative: it is the opposite of all that comes from God. And so we find certain characters in Spark's work mistakenly asserting themselves as the source of power and their own viewpoint as a criterion of truth. On the other hand we find characters who have a profound need to acknowledge a truth beyond themselves and who strive to come to terms with the essential inadequacy of a human perspective. These characters have a determination to identify what is true and honest in their existence; they have a sense of irony and sometimes a great sense of joy. All these characters describe themselves as Catholics. Although they are not portrayed as dependent on church ritual or practice, the dimension of faith is of the utmost importance to them.

Caroline in *The Comforters* is most explicitly bound up in her faith. She is a convert and finds herself patronized by cradle Catholics such as Mrs Hogg. She is irritated by this for she has a sense of her faith which lies beyond the smug platitudes of this woman. Although Caroline goes into retreat, she does not encounter her faith by turning her back on her life. On the contrary, the challenges, the irritations and the mysteries which nurture her faith are in her experience. She is aware that, unlike her friend Laurence, she is a wonderer; he either takes things for granted, or expects a technological solution. Caroline is ready to acquiesce before the pain and obscurity of her suffering; she has, it is said, a 'rapacity for suffering'. She has a fear of being artificially protected from truth; pain gives her a sense of the reality of existence and it is intensified as she offers it up to God. Although she calls the demands of Christianity exorbitant and outrageous, only through her faith can she find her true identity. Faith gives her the courage to face the strange things that are happening to her and although these frighten her, she will not deny them. She tells herself that she must not be tempted to deny the facts of her experience, since for a Catholic these are the provision of a privileged insight. Outsiders are sceptical about Caroline's faith, saying that she had 'little heart for it' and that her approach was intellectual. But it is clear to the reader that Caroline is involved with her faith on the same level as she is with her own experience. It provides its own demands and enables its own acquiescence.

Other characters who are also termed Catholics have less of a struggle as a result of their faith. They look to it for an endorsement of their understanding and for a reassurance in areas that they do not understand. Fleur Talbot in *Loitering with Intent* frequently declares that she has 'faith abounding'. She rejoices in existence more than any of Spark's other characters and this joy appears to be linked with her own creativity. She marvels at her good fortune at being an artist and a woman in the mid-twentieth century. However, this joy is not merely a personal ebullience. In terms of the narrative, Fleur's wellbeing is not presented solely as the consequence of her joy in her writing.

Fleur has a gift of perception; she can see clearly and is sensitive to the personalities of those around her. For example, she revels in the warmth and generosity of Edwina, Sir Quentin's aged mother, whom she treats with great respect. Sir Quentin's housekeeper derides Edwina and has nothing but contempt for her. Fleur is deeply suspicious of Sir Quentin although he charms and mystifies others. In addition to her sensitivity to the intrinsic character of others, Fleur is also able to evaluate and control herself. Although she has an aversion to both Mrs Tims, the housekeeper, and Dottie, the wife of her lover Leslie, she makes great efforts to compensate for these negative feelings. She gives Mrs Tims a brooch, she tries to help Dottie to find an interest in life by introducing her to the Autobiographical Association. However, Fleur herself is treated with deep distrust by all but her friends Leslie and Wally and by Edwina. She is accused of being unwomanly by Dottie and of being evil by Sir Quentin. Altogether the novel presents a spectrum of degrees of clarity and obscurity in appreciation of character. Fleur has the capacity to respond to the truth in people and has an aversion to pretentiousness and to inauthenticity. Her judgments are intuitive and she bears no malice and harbours no resentment. Her only anger results when she finds the typescript of her novel has been stolen, and even then her only desire is to reclaim it. She does not wish harm to the offenders. Basically her faith is reflected in her acknowledgement that life operates in terms beyond her understanding but that it offers a source of delight. She rejoices in her gift as a writer because to write celebrates what she observes and relishes as particular features of a personality or atmosphere. She rejoices 'in seeing people as they were and not only that but more than ever as they were and more and more'. It is clear that although Fleur is glad of her desire and ability to write, it is life itself that is the source of her joy. Although there is in the text no analysis of this in religious terms, the way in which Fleur's rejoicing connects with the quotations from Cellini and from Newman shows how she too is celebrating the truth. *Loitering with Intent* recounts a state of mind which is in itself an act of praise.

The faith of Nancy Hawkins in *A Far Cry from Kensington* is mentioned only incidentally. The insight of her faith comes into being in the course of the book. Initially it is no more in her life than a habit; we are told that she repeats the Angelus daily. However, when Nancy realizes how mistaken she has been about Wanda, the Polish dressmaker, she humbly adjusts her perspective. She sees, retrospectively, that a priest could have helped Wanda and protected her from the deceits of Hector Bartlett. Nancy's eventual readiness to admit to her own inadequacy is a strong feature of her Christian mentality. She compels herself to shake free of the identity into which she has sunk so comfortably and uses her free will to change her life. Like Fleur Talbot, Nancy has a clear appreciation of the personalities of others. But more importantly, she is able to criticize herself.

Barbara Vaughan in *The Mandelbaum Gate* has a different temperament from either Fleur Talbot or Nancy Hawkins. Her faith is the most passionate reality of her life. For her faith she uproots herself completely from her sheltered life as an English schoolteacher and embarks on a dangerous pilgrimage. Barbara has a good mind and a strong personality; her acquaintances find her daunting. But what emerges in this narrative is Barbara's need for a deeper level of existence. Barbara does not intellectualize this feeling. It is conveyed by the compulsion she has to pursue the pilgrimage, whatever the threats and difficulties. The priest who gives a sermon at the Holy Sepulchre offers insight into Barbara's experience; he says that to make a pilgrimage to Jerusalem is an instinct. He also says that the emotions aroused by it can vary, depending even on the weather. But what is essential is the disposition of the pilgrim. Even though the sites designated for reverence cannot all be authenticated: 'whether true or not our religion does not depend on it'. The certainty was that Christ died, was buried and rose again. 'The quest for historical exactitude belongs to archaeology not to faith,' says the friar and he continues: '... nothing is neat. And what would be the point of our professing faith if it were? There's no need for faith if everything is plain to the eye. We cannot know everything perfectly because we ourselves are not perfect.' The friars listening to the sermon are extremely uneasy about it; they see their fellow as a renegade and a firebrand. They know his views are likely to get him into trouble. Barbara is too feverish to pay much attention to his words. But for the reader they supply an unprecedented account of Spark's understanding of faith which is implicit throughout her work. Barbara is in fact the embodiment of what the priest is saying; she has an instinct and a longing to come to the Holy City and it is a spiritual need which nothing else in her life, not even her love affair, can satisfy. It is clear in her experience at the Eichmann trial how she sees in her pilgrimage terms of understanding which are inaccessible to the climate of cold bureaucracy at the trial and meaningless to the mechanical figure of Eichmann who raps out his pronouncements. The depths of suffering and the horror of the holocaust are of different dimension from these.

Caroline Rose, Fleur Talbot, Nancy Hawkins and Barbara Vaughan are comprehensible only in the terms they themselves present and these are the terms of their faith. No relationship and no preoccupation is as central to their lives as their need of an insight beyond what the world offers them. It is clear that for each of them faith proves a salutary force. It provides no answers, nor theoretical resolutions, but enables them to accept their limitations and the inadequacies of their understanding. The priest in his sermon at the Holy Sepulchre cites St Paul's definition of faith: 'It is that which gives substance to our hopes, which convinces us of things we cannot see.'

The characters I have presented as 'women of power' are remarkable for their lack of any faith beyond their self-love. This self-love separates them from others except for their need of acolytes. Selina Redwood in *The Girls of Slender Means* is a central character in the book only circumstantially. Her appalling selfishness emerges in its true light when she pushes past the trapped girls to retrieve the Schiaparelli dress. Without this revealing incident, her selfishness would have been socially tolerable, and barely noticed. However, it serves to offer a spiritual depth to the book which is no longer a pleasant, atmospheric account of young girls' adventures in wartime Britain. Selina's litany of dedication to perfect poise is sinister in retrospect rather than amusing. The effect that her action has on Nicholas changes his life. This is a subtle and profound way of indicating the spiritual significance of what initially appears to be an unimportant and inoffensive mentality.

Miss Brodie's preoccupation with self holds the centre of the stage. She is overwhelming because she admits no one's terms but her own. She is totally dismissive of others and entirely unselfcritical. Her favourite girls form an enchanted circle around her; they are admitted only because they acquiesce before her. She is grotesque; her inflated image of herself dominates all things. It is unwieldy and indefinable but its power is shown through the girls' excited fantasies and through the art master's inability to paint any face but hers. However, although she is obsessed with her own prejudices, there is a certain pathos about Miss Brodie. The irony of her outlook is that she sincerely believes she is doing the right thing. To her mind, her way of teaching is not showing off; she genuinely wishes to share with her girls the insights that she believes she has received. Her hostility to her critics amongst the staff of the Marcia Blaine School is not inspired by their dislike for her personally; she senses that they are philistines and that they seek to suppress all dynamism. The muddle of Miss Brodie's mind is amplified by the tensions of the time in which she lives. On the one hand there was an important movement in the thirties to celebrate art, health and unshackled learning. Many teachers and parents of the period must have felt that these were major issues to draw to the attention of the young. However, Miss Brodie's interest in such ideas is inseparable from her need of self-assertion. Because of this, she seeks to regiment the minds of those she teaches. Sandy's denunciation of her as a fascist is not so far removed from the truth. But Miss Brodie's confusion rambles further than the political. Her notion of her own power is almost deific. Not only does she seek to influence and channel her pupils and friends as a teacher, but she plans how they are to live and what they will do. It is here that she is most dangerous. Sandy is perceptive enough to see what Miss Brodie is trying to do. She betrays her. It is no coincidence that Sandy becomes a nun; faith and insight are linked. The other girls experience a great sense of freedom once they are no longer within Miss Brodie's control.

The narrator of *The Prime of Miss Jean Brodie* remarks that only the Catholic Church could have disciplined her 'soaring spirit'. She needs a sense of a power beyond her own so that she might orientate her enthusiasms and curb her egocentricity. Unwittingly, but dangerously, she takes people's lives into her own hands, denying them freedom. Her quest for power has taken away not only the freedom of others, but also her own: the concept of self as a prison emerges very clearly when, at the end of the day, we see her hunched, bedraggled and lonely, trying desperately to fathom out who betrayed her. Sandy points out that none of her girls could have betrayed her unless she had betrayed them; this was in fact what she had done.

Alexandra in *The Abbess of Crewe* is the epitome of cult of self. The irony of the narrative lies in the context of the abbey. Because of the implicit absence of any clear theological or moral ethos, the abbey only functions through an outmoded power structure. The junior nuns are servile, the older nuns assert their own will in a struggle for power. Alexandra has an obscure and mystifying personality. The reader has no insight into her thoughts. She is a law unto herself. She does not communicate with the other senior nuns; she declaims, they echo. She professes that her love is English poetry. Her devotions take the form of reciting the poetry of which she is so fond. She also claims to have an awareness of her own destiny. She knows she was meant to be Abbess. Alexandra is the antithesis of Christianity; she is exclusively preoccupied with herself, she is disdainful of others and wholly lacking in compassion, she has a Calvinist conviction of predestined outcome and a diabolic conviction that it is designed in her interests. As the narrative proceeds, we find other elements in her scheming which are equally tainted; the elaborate devices 'beyond the reach of any human vocabulary' enable Alexandra to operate a surveillance designed to protect her from any foe. She ably justifies these by quoting from the Scriptures: 'we must watch and pray'. She also quotes the practice of opening nuns' letters which she says is no less of an intrusion. After Felicity has escaped from the convent and Alexandra feels more threatened, she studies Machiavelli and gives passages of Machiavelli to the nuns to read aloud at mealtimes. Alexandra's nefarious scheming has become the *raison d'être* of the Abbey. It is a closed, suffocating environment. When she is called to Rome we see her on the ship and it seems that for once she has a sense of an infinity of possibilities beyond herself.

Spark's women of power ultimately prove to be vulnerable because they will admit no law beyond their own self-interest. Jean Brodie and Alexandra assert themselves to the exclusion of all other considerations. Their empire collapses. Selina Redwood is never consciously vulnerable; however, the perspective of the novel reveals the shallowness of her mind and her inability to foster relationships; the implication is that while she might enjoy worldly success, she is spiritually empty.

It is not only the personal experience of Spark's women nor their behaviour that suggests the value of a perspective of faith to assess them. In many of Spark's novels an alternative religion is often described. These are eccentric and often dangerous. Spark's skill in recounting the origins and effects of such cults shows her insight into the odd paths which a distorted religious sensibility may follow.

Spiritualism is portrayed in *The Bachelors*. In the structure of the novel it provides the means for Patrick Seton to manipulate his coterie. However, although Seton is undoubtedly presented as a malicious and scheming character, there is no suggestion in the text that his claim to be a medium is fraudulent. The description of his appearance and behaviour whilst going into a trance is clearly meant to convey a genuine state of semi-consciousness. He apparently has no recollection of what he says whilst in his trance. He knows that he has revealed something which profoundly disturbs Dr Lyte, but he has no idea what this was. He proceeds to use this revelation as blackmail against the doctor however. Having regained consciousness after one of his trances, he asks if he 'gave utterance'. All he had said, in fact, was 'I creep'. Patrick Seton's powers are sinister not laughable. The implication of the description of spiritualism in this book is that it does indeed tap sources which have a metaphysical reality, but that to exploit these is evil and chaotic. Ronald Bridges reflects that there are only two religions: spiritualism and Roman Catholicism. The latter provides the true points of reference to understand the forces of the spiritual dimension of existence.

Tom Wells in *Robinson* has his own superstitious cult. In his case it is quite clear that he preys for profit by marketing charms of his own invention: Ethel the Well is the most successful. This aspect of Tom Wells' character is abhorrent to January Marlow and also to Robinson himself. He is deeply irritated by Tom Wells' attempt to interest Miguel, Robinson's step son, in his superstitious object. Interestingly, Robinson also objects to January's rosary beads and is offended when she teaches the rosary to Miguel.

Muriel Spark's impatience with mindless religiosity is clear from the way in which she derides superstition of the kind encouraged by Tom Wells. She is equally scathing about the macrobiotics cult of Lise's fellow passenger, Bill. One has the impression that Spark is not mocking these characters merely on a personal level but that she is genuinely affronted by the way in which a human tendency towards religion can be distorted and corrupted. In *The Takeover* this criticism is most fully developed. Hubert Mallindaine attempts to revive a cult of the goddess Diana from whom he claims to be descended. This claim, it is pointed out, has no firmer basis than the sentimentality of his maiden aunts. It does appear that Hubert himself has an emotional conviction that he has the right to a form of priesthood because of his ancestry; talking to himself, he declares that the whole area is his because it was originally dedicated to the worship of Diana.

153

Like Spark's other characters who pursue eccentric religious cults, Hubert has an eye to profit. He has no compunction in having made faked copies of Maggie's possessions and selling the originals. He too has an obsession about his own supremacy; when praying, he simply assumes God will be persuaded what to do by him. Spark wickedly suggests that many other ministers have a similar approach and regard their self-interest as a valid factor in the operation of God's will. But her real target is the charismatic movement in the Roman Catholic Church. Hubert's ability to assemble congregations who enjoy the egalitarian atmosphere of the cult and his fuzzy, histrionic nature worship, is really a form of theatre. It is basically phoney and has only a contagious emotive content. Spark implies that the charismatic movement in the Church is similar; people enjoy a relaxed, friendly atmosphere to get away from confronting the realities of life.

Muriel Spark does not write theology. There is no attempt to write a résumé nor to analyse the nature or function of religion. She does, however, identify an area in human experience which relates to faith; this area is where the building of a true human identity takes place. Spark's characters do not develop in terms of their relationships with others, but in terms of their own encounters with challenge. Her presentation of life suggests an essential fragmentation, an essential incoherence. Sometimes, in order to show how substanceless is a reliance on the predictable, Spark uses an author's licence in giving her narrative a surrealist, metaphysical dimension. The disappearance of Mrs Hogg, when alone, is an example. The strange links between Fleur Talbot's novel and the events of Sir Quentin's life are another. Such themes are deliberately left unresolved. We are encouraged to think that 'all things are possible'. This, the novelist has the right to suggest, is what faith encourages.

The most impressive account of essential incoherence is that of the personal experience of Spark's characters. The maturing woman is able to cope with this through her faith. The woman seeking power dismisses incoherence and blurs this reality with myth. Such a quest emerges as highly comic, not just on the level of circumstances and unpredictable events, but as the result of the irony of the absolute imposition of an arbitrary and partial set of criteria.

The faith which figures so essentially in Spark's writing is not presented as an orthodox Roman Catholicism. There is little reference to following regular religious practices; when there is – for example, January Marlow's rosary, Nancy Hawkins' recitation of the Angelus – these tend to be the object of mockery, rather than to suggest piety. There are some Catholics whose understanding of the faith is presented as quite obnoxious: Mrs Hogg in *The Comforters* and Dottie in *Loitering with Intent*. Fleur Talbot says of Dottie's faith that she was rather glad when she said she had lost it since she felt that if Dottie's faith was the true faith, then hers was false. Clearly, a veneer or a pretence of faith is as reprehensible as any other inauthenticity. Muriel Spark's respect for authenticity appears to be one of the essential criteria for faith. The characters she presents in the most sympathetic light have a high standard of honesty and integrity. Those openly reviled by Spark's narrative are fraudulent. They manipulate others and are nefarious and dishonest.

It would be quite wrong to interpret the elements of criticism of the Catholic Church in Spark's work as an indication that there is a waning of the importance of faith in her outlook. Her focus on life is witty and ironic because she refuses to present it as comprehensible in its entirety. Occasionally, such as in the Scripture readings in *The Abbess of Crewe* and in the Biblical quotations read out at one of Hubert Mallandaine's cult services by his secretary, there is a direct attempt to provide the reader with suggestions of an alternative perspective to that of the characters. But mostly Spark trusts that the very presentation of a fragmentary and bafflingly mysterious life will awake in the reader an admission that we see through a glass darkly. She expresses this perception with the rhythms and the imagery of poetry to confer on it a wonder of its own.

Index

156

Index

157

Index